T0324778

Data Mining for Bioinformatics Applications

Related titles

From plant genomics to plant biotechnology
(ISBN: 978-1-907568-29-9)

An introduction to biotechnology
(ISBN: 978-1-907568-28-2)

MATLABs in bioscience and biotechnology
(ISBN: 978-1-907568-04-6)

Woodhead Publishing Series in Biomedicine: Number 76

Data Mining for Bioinformatics Applications

Zengyou He

AMSTERDAM • BOSTON • CAMBRIDGE • HEIDELBERG
LONDON • NEW YORK • OXFORD • PARIS • SAN DIEGO
SAN FRANCISCO • SINGAPORE • SYDNEY • TOKYO

Woodhead Publishing is an imprint of Elsevier

Woodhead Publishing Limited is an imprint of Elsevier
80 High Street, Sawston, Cambridge, CB22 3HJ, UK
225 Wyman Street, Waltham, MA 02451, USA
Langford Lane, Kidlington, OX5 1GB, UK

Notices
Knowledge and best practice in this field are constantly changing. As new research and experience broaden our understanding, changes in research methods, professional practices, or medical treatment may become necessary.

Practitioners and researchers must always rely on their own experience and knowledge in evaluating and using any information, methods, compounds, or experiments described herein. In using such information or methods they should be mindful of their own safety and the safety of others, including parties for whom they have a professional responsibility.

To the fullest extent of the law, neither the Publisher nor the authors, contributors, or editors, assume any liability for any injury and/or damage to persons or property as a matter of products liability, negligence or otherwise, or from any use or operation of any methods, products, instructions, or ideas contained in the material herein.

ISBN: 978-0-08-100100-4 (print)
ISBN: 978-0-08-100107-3 (online)

British Library Cataloguing-in-Publication Data
A catalogue record for this book is available from the British Library

Library of Congress Control Number: 2015934370

For information on all Woodhead Publishing publications
visit our website at http://store.elsevier.com/

Working together
to grow libraries in
developing countries

www.elsevier.com • www.bookaid.org

Contents

List of figures

List of tables

About the author

Zengyou He is an associate professor in the School of Software at Dalian University of Technology, China.

He received his BS, MS, and PhD degrees in computer science from the Harbin Institute of Technology, China, in 2000, 2002, and 2006, respectively. Prior to becoming an associate professor, he was a research associate in the Department of Electronic and Computer Engineering at the Hong Kong University of Science and Technology (2007–2010).

His research interests include computational proteomics and biological data mining. He has published more than 30 papers on leading journals in the field of bioinformatics, including *Bioinformatics*, *BMC Bioinformatics*, *Briefings in Bioinformatics*, *IEEE/ACM Transactions on Computational Biology and Bioinformatics*, and *Journal of Computational Biology*.

Dedication

Introduction

Data mining methods have been widely used for solving real bioinformatics problems. However, the data mining process is not trivial. It consists of many steps: problem definition, data collection, data preprocessing, modeling, and validation. For each step, different techniques may be applied. Due to the complexity of data mining process and data mining methods, people cannot easily use data mining tools to solve their bioinformatics problems.

In this book, I will use an example-based method to illustrate how to apply data mining techniques to solving real bioinformatics problems. More precisely, I will use six bioinformatics problems that have been investigated in my recent research as examples. For each example, I will describe the entire data mining process, ranging from data preprocessing to modeling and result validation. In addition, I will describe how to use *different* data mining methods to solve the *same* bioinformatics problem in some examples.

In this problem-driven book, I will cover the most commonly used data mining methods, such as frequent pattern mining, discriminative pattern mining, classification, and clustering to show how to select one feasible data mining method to solve a real bioinformatics problem at hand.

Audience

This book will have obvious appeal for a broad audience of computer scientists who are interested in designing new data mining algorithms and biologists who are trying to solve bioinformatics problems using existing data mining tools. To achieve this objective, this book is organized with the following distinct features.

- Providing an example-based description on the whole data mining process for bioinformatics applications. This is distinct from method-based description, in which the chapters are organized according to different data mining techniques. Such an example-based organization is beneficial as it may help the readers to understand how to solve a real problem at hand by choosing proper data mining methods.
- Covering most popular data mining techniques throughout the book. Currently, there are many data mining methods in the literature. This book covers most of them and shows their applications in practical bioinformatics problems.
- Giving detailed illustrations and examples of how to use different data mining techniques to solve the same bioinformatics problem. Due to the complex nature of bioinformatics problems, the same problem can be solved using different data mining techniques. Different

solutions vary from underlying assumptions to algorithmic details. Such kinds of examples will not only enable the reader to understand the target problem more deeply, but also provide hints on how to apply data mining methods in his or her future bioinformatics research.
- Using frontier bioinformatics problems as examples in each chapter. All the examples discussed in this book will be frontier bioinformatics problems that are under investigation by the author and other researchers. Students who are interested in developing new and better algorithms for these problems may use this book as a starting point.

Acknowledgments

Many articles and books have been referenced in the writing of this book, and citations have been given for these works. To enhance the readability, I have tried to minimize literature references in the text. The sources and some additional literature that may be interesting to the readers are included in the reference section at the end of each chapter. I hope that this organization will provide the authors of the source literature with the appropriate acknowledgments. Moreover, this work was partially supported by the Natural Science Foundation of China under the Grant No. 61003176, the Fundamental Research Funds for the Central Universities of China under the Grant No. DUT14QY07.

This book could not have been written without the help of many people. First of all, most contents in this book are based on the research articles coauthored by my students and myself. Therefore, I would like to first thank my former and current students: Ting Huang, Haipeng Gong, Yang Zhang, Ben Teng, Xiaoqing Liu, Jun Wu, Can Zhao, and Feiyang Gu. In particular, I am grateful to Ben Teng and Xiaoqing Liu, who have carefully read the book and given very detailed comments and suggestions.

In addition, I would like to thank my former colleagues at the Hong Kong University of Science and Technology: Weichuan Yu, Can Yang, Chao Yang, and Xiang Wan, who have assisted me with the study of bioinformatics problems that have contributed to this book.

Furthermore, I am especially thankful to my PhD supervisor, Professor Xiaofei Xu, for his continuous efforts on "transforming" my research style from algorithm-driven research to application-driven research. Without such a transition, I would not have been able to write and finish this book.

Last, but definitely not least, I am indebted to my parents, my wife, and my son for their continuous support and patience.

Zengyou He
Dalian, China

An overview of data mining

1

1.1 What's data mining?

Data mining lies at the intersection of computer science, optimization, and statistics, and often appears in other disciplines. Generally, data mining is the process of searching for knowledge in data from different perspectives. Here knowledge can refer to any kinds of summarized or unknown information that are hidden underlying the raw data. For instance, it can be a set of discriminative rules generated from the data collected on some patients of a certain disease and healthy people. These rules can be used for predicting the disease status of new patients.

In general, data mining tasks can be classified into two categories: *descriptive* and *predictive*. Descriptive mining tasks characterize a target data set in concise, informative, discriminative forms. Predictive mining tasks conduct the induction and inference on the current data to make future predictions.

1.2 Data mining process models

Data mining is an iterative process that consists of many steps. There are already some generic reference models on the data mining process, such as the Cross Industry Standard Process for Data Mining (CRISP-DM) process model. From a data-centric perspective, these models are structured as sequences of steps to transform the raw data into information or knowledge that is practically useful. As shown in Figure 1.1, a data mining process model typically involves the following phases: data collection, data preprocessing, data modeling, model assessment, and model deployment.

1.3 Data collection

The first step in the data mining process is to collect the relevant data according to the analysis goal in the applications. Generally, all the data that are helpful to achieve the objective in the analysis should be included. The key point here is how to define and understand the rather subjective term of "relevant data." Its correct interpretation highly depends on our understanding of the target problem and application background. Although this point will be further illustrated in subsequent chapters, we offer some general remarks here:

- In some cases, people definitely know that some kinds of data are highly relevant to the data mining task at hand. However, the acquisition of such data is very difficult or even impossible due to the device deficiency or cost. For instance, to accurately identify peptides in mass-spectrometry-based shotgun proteomics, it is necessary to generate at least one mass

Data Mining for Bioinformatics Applications. http://dx.doi.org/10.1016/B978-0-08-100100-4.00001-6

Figure 1.1 Typical phases involved in a data mining process model.

spectrum for each peptide in the sample. However, due to the limitation of current mass spectrometers, it is not always possible to obtain mass spectra data that can cover all peptides present in the sample.
- On the other hand, the inclusion of new relevant data may significantly change the models and methods in the consequent steps of the data mining process. Furthermore, it is necessary to check thoroughly if the use of more relevant data will boost the performance of data mining procedures.

1.4   Data preprocessing

The objective of data preprocessing is twofold: (1) The real-world data are usually low quality; hence preprocessing is used to improve the quality of data, and consequently, the quality of data mining results. (2) In the data modeling step, some specific modeling algorithms cannot operate on the raw data, which should be transformed into some predefined data formats.

There are several general-purpose data preprocessing methods: *data cleaning*, *data integration*, *data reduction,* and *data transformation*.

Data cleaning: Real-world data are usually noisy, inconsistent, and incomplete. Data cleaning procedures aim at removing the noise, correcting inconsistencies, and filling in missing values in the data.

Data integration: In the data collection phase, data sets from different sources are relevant to the analysis problem. Data integration merges data from different sources into an integrated data set for subsequent data mining analysis. The main objective of data integration is to reduce and avoid redundancies and inconsistencies in the resulting data set.

Data reduction: The purpose of data reduction is to generate a new yet smaller representation of the original data set. Generally, the reduced data should contain approximately the same information of the original data that is of primary importance to the analysis target. The most commonly used data reduction technique includes dimension reduction (vertically, reduce the number of features) and sampling (horizontally, reduce the number of samples).

Data transformation: Different data mining algorithms may require different forms of data. Data transformation techniques consolidate the original data into forms appropriate for subsequent mining tasks. For instance, data normalization will transform the feature values into a predefined range such as [0.0, 1.0]. Data discretization will replace a continuous feature with a discrete one by dividing numeric values into intervals.

1.5 Data modeling

Before discussing the data modeling algorithms, it would be best to explain some terminology. Typically, the data preprocessing step would transform the raw data into a tabular form, in which the columns represent features/variables and rows correspond to samples/instances. For instance, Table 1.1 is a sample data set that has eight samples and five features (class is a special feature for which we are aiming to predict its feature value for a new given sample). The first four features are called *predictive features* and the class feature is the *target feature*. Here the predictive features can be symptoms of some disease, where the value of 1 indicates the existence of a symptom and 0 indicates otherwise. Similarly, the class feature value is 1 if the corresponding person (sample) has the disease.

1.5.1 Pattern mining

Pattern discovery is a core data mining problem, which generates a set of interesting patterns that characterize the data sets in concise and informative forms. Initially, the studies on pattern discovery were dominated by the frequent pattern discovery paradigm, where only frequent patterns were explored. Currently, the issue of frequent pattern discovery has been thoroughly investigated, rendering its limitations well understood. Many alternative pattern discovery formulations are emerging and investigated in the literature. For example, many research efforts impose statistical significance tests over candidate patterns to control the risk of false discoveries.

Table 1.1 **An example data set with eight samples and five features**

	Feature 1	Feature 2	Feature 3	Feature 4	Class
1	0	0	1	1	0
2	0	1	1	1	0
3	1	0	0	1	0
4	1	0	0	0	0
5	1	1	1	1	1
6	1	1	1	1	1
7	0	0	1	1	1
8	1	1	0	0	1

Here *class* is a special feature representing the category to which each sample belongs.

Let $D = \{t_1, t_2, \ldots, t_n\}$ be a data set, and each t_i is an instance or sample and each sample has g features $f_1, f_2, \ldots, f_g$. For ease of illustration, all features are assumed to be categorical. An item is defined as a feature-value pair $f_i = v$, where v is one of feature values taken from f_i. One sample contains an item $f_i = v$ if it takes v as its feature value for the feature f_i. The universe of all possible items that occur in the data set is denoted as $I = \{i_1, i_2, \ldots, i_m\}$.

In the example of Table 1.1, "Feature $1 = 0$" and "Feature $1 = 1$" are two items that are derived from the first feature.

A pattern $p = \{i_1, i_2, \ldots, i_k\}$ is a subset of all items, that is, $p \subseteq I$. p is defined as a k-pattern if it is composed of k items. For example, {"Feature $3 = 1$," "Feature $4 = 1$"} is a 2-pattern since it has two items.

A sample contains a pattern p if all items in p appear in that sample. For instance, the pattern {"Feature $3 = 1$," "Feature $4 = 1$"} is contained in the first, second, fifth, sixth, and seventh sample, respectively.

To date, there are many different methods for evaluating the interestingness of each pattern. Different interestingness evaluation methods lead to different pattern discovery problems. Generally, it is reasonable to assume that there is a generic interestingness calculation function $E(p)$, which can take different forms. For example, the popular frequent pattern discovery problem is based on the following pattern evaluation approach:

$$E(p) = \frac{|\{t_i | p \subseteq t_i\}|}{n}, \tag{1.1}$$

where n is the number of samples in the data set and $|\cdot|$ represents the size of a set.

In the context of frequent pattern discovery, the value $E(p)$ is defined as the "support" of pattern p. Clearly, the support of a pattern is the percentage of samples that contain this pattern in a data set. For instance, the support for pattern {"Feature $3 = 1$," "Feature $4 = 1$"} in Table 1.1 is 5/8.

A pattern is frequent if its support value is no less than a user-defined threshold. The problem of frequent pattern mining is to find all frequent patterns. Suppose the minimum support threshold is specified to be 0.5, then {"Feature $3 = 1$," "Feature $4 = 1$"} in Table 1.1 is a frequent pattern since $5/8 > 0.5$.

To effectively identify frequent patterns, a large number of algorithms have been proposed over the last 20 years. Among these methods, the most well-known algorithms are Apriori and FP-growth, which traverse the pattern space in a breadth-first manner and a depth-first manner, respectively.

Apriori iteratively enumerates and checks all frequent patterns based on the antimonotonic property, that is, if a pattern is frequent, then all of its subpatterns must also be frequent. More precisely, the set of frequent patterns of size one is first generated by scanning the data set. When generating frequent patterns of size k, the following steps are performed:

1. Generate the set of potential frequent patterns of size k by combining two patterns from the set of frequent patterns of size $k - 1$. Two patterns are said to be joinable if their first $k - 2$ items are the same.

2. Calculate the support of each candidate pattern of size k. Prune all the infrequent ones and add all the left to the set of frequent k-patterns.
3. Repeat the above steps until no more frequent candidates can be generated.

FP-growth adopts a divide-and-conquer strategy to discover all frequent patterns without candidate generation by constructing a frequent pattern tree (FP-tree). An FP-tree (frequent pattern tree) is a variation of the tree data structure, which is a prefix-tree structure for storing the crucial and compressed information about the support. It is composed of one root labeled as "NULL," a set of item prefix subtrees as the children of the root, and a frequent item header table. Each node in the item prefix subtree has three fields: *item-name*, *count*, and *node-link*, where *item-name* is the item name that this node represents, *count* is the number of samples that contains items in the portion of the path reaching this node, and *node-link* links to the next node in the FP-tree carrying the same item-name, or null if there is none. Each entry in the frequent item header table has two fields: *item name* and *head of node-link*. The *head of node-link* points to the first node in the FP-tree carrying the item name.

After the FP-tree is constructed, FP-growth identifies frequent patterns directly from the FP-tree as follows. Initially, each frequent pattern of size one is used as the suffix pattern. Then, the conditional pattern base of each suffix pattern is constructed as the set of prefix paths in the FP-tree cooccurring with this suffix pattern. From the conditional pattern base, a conditional FP-tree is generated for the suffix pattern. The above procedure is performed recursively on the conditional FP-tree. The so-called pattern growth is achieved by the concatenation of the suffix pattern with the frequent patterns generated from the conditional FP-tree.

It is well recognized that the true correlation relationship among items or features may be missed in the support-based pattern discovery framework. Therefore, people have begun to study alternative pattern discovery formulations that use the statistical correlation measures to evaluate the interestingness of patterns. For example, the ϕ correlation coefficient (the computation form of the Pearson's correlation coefficient for binary variables) can be adopted for measuring the correlation between two items of a pattern $p = \{i_1, i_2\}$, that is,

$$E(p) = \phi(i_1, i_2) = \frac{\sup(i_1, i_2) - \sup(i_1)\sup(i_2)}{\sqrt{\sup(i_1)\sup(i_2)(1 - \sup(i_1))(1 - \sup(i_1))}}, \qquad (1.2)$$

where $\sup(i_1)$, $\sup(i_2)$, and $\sup(i_1, i_2)$ denote the support values of item(s) i_1, i_2, and $\{i_1, i_2\}$, respectively.

The correlation mining can be used for evaluating the association relationship of features rather than items as well. The basic idea is to adopt a correlation measure that is capable of measuring the association for nonbinary categorical features or numeric features.

The pattern discovery problems discussed above are unsupervised; that is, the special-class feature is not considered in the pattern evaluation. Indeed, the discovery of distinguishing characteristics between different classes is one of the most important objectives in data mining as well. The objective of discriminative pattern mining is to find a set of patterns that occur with disproportionate frequency in one class versus others.

To evaluate the discriminative power of one pattern, one common strategy is to evaluate the difference of its support values across different classes. A wide variety of evaluation measures are available for this purpose. For instance, the absolute difference of supports is one of the simplest measures for evaluating the discriminative power in a two-class context:

$$E(p) = |\sup^{(1)}(p) - \sup^{(2)}(p)|, \qquad (1.3)$$

where $\sup^{(i)}(p)$ represents the support of pattern p in the set of samples that belong to the ith class ($i = 1, 2$). Given a user-specified threshold, if the value of discriminative measure can pass the threshold, then the pattern is claimed to be a discriminative pattern.

In the example data set of Table 1.1, the supports of {"Feature $1 = 1$," "Feature $2 = 1$"} are 0 and 3/4 in the class labeled as "0" and "1," respectively. According to the formula (1.3), their absolute support difference is $|0 - 0.75| = 0.75$. Clearly, this pattern has an apparent frequency difference between two classes.

Discriminative pattern mining is more computationally challenging than frequent pattern mining. This is because most discriminative measures do not have the antimonotonic property. Therefore, discriminative pattern-mining algorithms usually adopt a two-stage procedure: first generate a set of frequent patterns, and then evaluate the discriminative power of each frequent pattern. Alternatively, one can also design approaches for mining discriminative patterns by discovering significant discriminative patterns in a single step.

1.5.2 Supervised predictive modeling: Classification and regression

Supervised learning aims at building a predictive model from the data when a class/target feature is available. There are two types of class features: categorical features and numeric features. The categorical feature can take only nominal values, whereas the numeric feature can take an infinite number of numeric values. Generally, the predictive model is called *classification model* and *regression model* when the class feature is categorical and numeric, respectively. In other words, classification is to predict what category a sample should fall into while regression is the prediction of a numeric value. Here "supervised" means that the algorithm is aware of what to predict because class feature is specified.

In both classification and regression, the training data are used to build the predictive model and the testing data are used to evaluate the performance.

There are numerous classification algorithms in the literature, which belong to different "classifier families." That is, these classification methods arise from different fields within computer science and mathematics. For example, the linear discriminant analysis comes from statistics, rule-based classifiers or decision trees come from artificial intelligence and data mining, and so forth. In a recent study [1], 179 classifiers arising from 17 families were empirically compared over 121 data sets. It shows that the classifiers most likely to be the best are random forest (RF) and support vector machine (SVM). These two methods are briefly introduced in the following.

RF is widely used in bioinformatics applications because RF classification models have high prediction accuracy and can provide additional information such as the feature importance. RF is an ensemble of individual decision trees, where each tree in the forest is constructed with a random subset of samples and features. To predict the class of a new sample, every decision tree in the forest casts an unweighted vote for the sample after which the majority vote determines the class of the sample.

SVM is one of most well-known classifiers, which has a sound theoretical foundation. In a two-class classification task (one class is defined as the *positive class* and another class is referred to as the *negative class*), the aim of SVM is to find a classification function that is able to distinguish between samples of the two classes in the training data. Geometrically, if the samples from two classes can be linearly separated, the classification function $f(x)$ is linear that corresponds to a separating hyperplane that passes through the middle of the two classes. Once this function is generated, a new data sample x_n can be classified by simply testing the sign of the function. That is, the new data sample will be assigned to the positive class if $f(x_n) > 0$. Otherwise, this sample will be assigned to the negative class.

Under the assumption that samples from two classes are linearly separable, there will be many linear functions that can achieve the above objective. Therefore, SVM requires that this function should be able to maximize the margin between the two classes. Geometrically, the margin corresponds to the shortest distance between the closest data samples to a sample on the hyperplane. This concept of margin enables us to formulate the classifier construction problem as an optimization problem, where the objective is to maximize the margin under the constraints that samples from two classes are separable. It has been argued that the generation of maximum margin hyperplanes can offer good generalization ability (the ability of correct classification of the future data).

The above fundamental formulation of SVM is based on a few unrealistic assumptions such as the data samples from different classes are linearly separable. To make it feasible for real-world classification problems, some extensions have been made. First, the "soft margin" idea is proposed to extend the SVM optimization model so that the classification function allows the existence of a few data samples of the opposite classes that cross the function. In addition, to handle the situations where the training data are not linearly separable, the kernel trick is used to transform the data from the original feature space into another high-dimensional feature space.

For the task of regression, the most popular methods are linear regression and its variants. In linear regression, a linear equation is constructed from the training data with the regression weights as the unknown parameters. Once the regression weights are obtained, the class feature value for a new sample can be forecasted.

In many bioinformatics applications, there are always data sets that have more features than data samples. In this case, it is not feasible to make a prediction using the standard linear regression method. To solve this problem, statisticians introduced so-called shrinkage methods such as *Lasso*, which are variants of linear regression by imposing some additional constraints.

In Lasso regression, the sum of the absolute values of all weights has to be less than or equal to a user-specified parameter. Subject to this constraint, some weight coefficients are forced to be exactly zeros if that parameter is small enough. This nice property makes it possible to eliminate irrelevant features in high-dimensional data sets.

1.5.3   Unsupervised descriptive modeling: Cluster analysis

The opposite of supervised learning is the problem of unsupervised learning, where the class feature is unavailable for the data. A fundamental unsupervised learning task is clustering or cluster analysis, which partitions data samples into different groups. The generic clustering criteria are twofold: (1) data samples in the same group are similar and (2) data samples from different groups are dissimilar.

There are many clustering algorithms in the literature. In general, these clustering methods can be classified into different categories. Among existing clustering algorithms, the most widely used methods are partitioning methods and hierarchical methods. The partitioning methods generate a one-level partitioning on data sets whereas the hierarchical methods create a hierarchical decomposition of the data samples.

The k-means algorithm is the most popular clustering method, which is a partitioning algorithm that will generate k clusters for a given data set. The number of clusters k is a user-specified parameter. Each cluster is represented by a single data point known as the *centroid*. A centroid is the center of all the data samples in the cluster.

In the k-means algorithm, k centroids are randomly generated in the first step. Then, each data sample in the data set is assigned to the closest cluster according the distance between the data sample and the corresponding centroid. After this step, each centroid is updated as the new mean value of all the samples in that cluster.

Since the k-means algorithm can handle only numeric data sets, the k-modes algorithm extends the k-means paradigm to cluster categorical data by using (1) a simple matching distance measure for categorical data, (2) modes instead of means as the centroids for clusters, and (3) a frequency-based method to update modes in the k-means fashion to minimize the cost function of clustering.

1.6   Model assessment

The assessment of data mining results is extremely important in practice, because it guides the choice of models and measures the quality of the ultimately chosen model. It is important to note that models and patterns learned from the training data by the data mining algorithms are not necessarily valid, which may not be present in the future data set.

To validate the data mining results, there are different strategies for different data mining tasks. For the task of supervised predictive modeling, the evaluation generally uses a testing data set on which the learning algorithm was not trained. For the task of unsupervised descriptive modeling, statistical testing methods are usually adopted to evaluate the significance of discovered patterns or knowledge. The details of different validation methods will be presented in the corresponding chapters.

If the learned knowledge or models do not meet the desired standards, subsequently it is necessary to re-evaluate and change the preprocessing and data mining steps.

1.7 Model deployment

Extensive research efforts in data mining have been done on discovering knowledge from the underlying data. Despite such phenomenal success, most of these techniques stop short of the final objective of data mining—providing possible actions to maximize the profit while reducing costs for the end users. Although these techniques are essential to moving the data mining results to the eventual application, they nevertheless require a great deal of expert manuals to postprocess mined knowledge. Overall, the model deployment by taking actions to make a profit for individuals or organizations is the ultimate goal of data mining. For instance, discriminative patterns discovered from the case–control studies must be linked to their biological interpretations to facilitate the clinical validation.

From a computational perspective, making the mined patterns or knowledge *actionable* is critical to facilitate the model deployment. Here, the term *actionable* means that the learned model or patterns should suggest concrete and profitable actions to the decision maker. That is, the user can *do* something to bring direct benefits (increase in profits, reduction in cost, improvement in efficiency, etc.) to the organization's advantage.

To make the mined model and patterns actionable, one typical strategy is to integrate the data mining process into the decision process. This requires a deep understanding of the application problem and related background knowledge. Therefore, the problem of model deployment is quite complicated and cooperation from multiple disciplines is highly demanded.

1.8 Summary

Data mining is already being successfully used in different real-life applications. In this chapter, key data mining concepts and tasks are introduced. For further reading, we suggest two textbooks. For nonprofessionals, Ref. [2] is a good choice as it introduces data mining and machine learning techniques in an easy-to-understand manner. For others who want more technical details, another popular data mining textbook [3] is recommended.

References

[1] M. Fernández-Delgado, E. Cernadas, S. Barro, D. Amorim, Do we need hundreds of classifiers to solve real world classification problems? J. Mach. Learn. Res. 15 (2014) 3133–3181.
[2] P. Harrington, Machine Learning in Action, Manning Publications Co., Greenwich, CT, 2012.
[3] J. Han, M. Kamber, J. Pei, Data Mining: Concepts and Techniques, third ed., Morgan Kaufmann, Waltham, MA, 2012.

Introduction to bioinformatics

2

2.1 A primer to molecular biology

To understand bioinformatics, it is necessary to have a rudimentary grasp of biology. This section gives a brief introduction to some basic concepts of molecular biology that are relevant to the bioinformatics problems discussed in later chapters.

The *cell* is the basic unit of life. Despite of the diversity of cells, they all have a life cycle: they are born, eat, replicate, and die. During the life cycle, a cell makes different decisions through the manifestation in pathways.

Three types of basic molecules are present in a cell: deoxyribonucleic acid (DNA), ribonucleic acid (RNA), and proteins. Intuitively, DNA, RNA, and proteins can be viewed as strings. DNA is a very long molecule that is composed of four types of bases: adenine (A), thymine (T), guanine (G), and cytosine (C). Similar to DNA, there are four bases in RNA as well. The major difference is that the T base is replaced by the base uracil (U) in RNA. Each protein is a string sequence consisting of 20 types of amino acids.

DNA carries the genetic information of a cell and is composed of thousands of genes. Every cell contains the genetic information so that the DNA is duplicated before a cell divides (*replication*). When proteins are needed, the corresponding genes are transcribed into RNA (*transcription*). Therefore, RNA's primary responsibility is to synthesize the particular protein according to the protein-encoding information within the DNA (*translation*). Proteins are responsible for performing biochemical reactions, sending signals to other cells, and forming the body's major components.

Overall, DNA makes RNA, and then RNA makes proteins. This information flow,

$$\textbf{DNA} \rightarrow \textit{transcription} \rightarrow \textbf{RNA} \rightarrow \textit{translation} \rightarrow \textbf{protein},$$

is often referred to as the *central dogma in molecular biology*.

2.2 What is bioinformatics?

Bioinformatics is an interdisciplinary field that develops computational methods and software packages for analyzing biological data. As an interdisciplinary field of science, bioinformatics combines technologies from computer science, statistics, and optimization to process biological data. The ultimate goal of bioinformatics is to discover new biological insights through the analysis of biological data.

Currently, a general pipeline for addressing a science problem in bioinformatics is as follows [1]:

1. Wet labs design experiments and prepare samples.
2. Large amount of biological data are generated.

Data Mining for Bioinformatics Applications. http://dx.doi.org/10.1016/B978-0-08-100100-4.00002-8

3. Existing (or new) computational and statistical methods are applied (or developed).
4. Data analysis results are further validated by wet lab testing.
5. If necessary, the procedure of 1–4 is repeated with refinements.

However, the bioinformatics research often reflects a two-sided problem [1]: (1) Researchers in computer science and other related fields just regard bioinformatics as one specific application of their theories and methods due to the inability to provide precise solutions to complex molecular biology problems. (2) Biologists focus on hypothesis testing of wet labs so that bioinformatics serves as a tool for analyzing the biological data generated from their experiments.

It is not difficult to see that both sides have their own limitations. Computational scientists need to have a good understanding of biology and biomedical sciences, whereas biologists need to better understand the nature of their data analysis problem from an algorithmic perspective. Therefore, the lack of integration of these two sides not only limits the development of life science research, but also limits the development of computational methods in bioinformatics.

2.3   Data mining issues in bioinformatics

In recent years, rapid developments in genomics and proteomics have produced a large amount of biological data from wet labs in different formats. Data mining approaches are ideally suited for data-rich bioinformatics applications, where enormous amounts of data need to be analyzed to solve the puzzles of life. Drawing scientific conclusions from the biological data requires the application and development of data mining techniques in a right way.

However, it is vital to examine what are the important research issues in bioinformatics. There is no doubt that the objective of research is to address scientific challenges. Therefore, the real challenges in bioinformatics are how to solve the scientific issues rather than focusing too heavily on collecting and analyzing biological data. In other words, bioinformatics research ought to be science driven instead of data driven.

Because of the complexity of life's organization, there are numerous challenging research issues in bioinformatics. Thus, it is very hard to provide a complete categorization of bioinformatics problems. Generally, data analysis-related problems in bioinformatics can be divided into three classes according to the type of biological data: *sequences, structures,* and *networks.*

2.3.1   Sequences

The sequences of DNA, RNA, and protein are of primary importance in life science. Many bioinformatics problems that focus on the studies of sequences, which can be roughly classified into three categories: (1) *the analysis and comparison of multiple sequences,* (2) *sequence identification from experimental data,* and (3) *sequence classification and regression.*

2.3.1.1 The analysis and comparison of multiple sequences

The analysis and comparison of multiple biological sequences has become a fundamental bioinformatics issue in many different domains in modern molecular biology, whose applications range from evolutionary studies to the prediction of molecular functions and intermolecular interactions, among others. The key issue to be addressed is to find patterns or structures from a given set of biological sequences. There are many variants of such sequence analysis and comparison problems. Among these problems, multiple sequence alignment and motif discovery are probably two of the most important bioinformatics problems in the literature.

Multiple sequence alignment: A sequence alignment is a way of arranging the biological sequences to identify similar regions that may be a consequence of functional, structural, or evolutionary relationships among the sequences. Aligned sequences are typically represented as rows within a matrix, where gaps are inserted so that identical or similar characters are aligned in successive columns. There are numerous methods for aligning multiple sequences, such as Clustal W, Muscle, T-Coffee, Dialign, Mafft, DCA, and ProbCons. Figure 2.1 presents an example of multiple sequence alignment, where five biological sequences are aligned together.

Motif discovery: Motif discovery is an important bioinformatics problem with numerous applications. Generally, a sequence motif is a nucleotide or amino-acid sequence pattern that is widespread and has a biological significance. Given a set of biological sequences, the motif discovery is to find a set of motifs, where each motif satisfies the given criteria. There are different problem formulations for motif discovery in different domains, ranging from regulatory DNA motif to posttranslational modification (PTM) motif of proteins. The discovery of phosphorylation motif, which is one particular and important PTM motif, is discussed in detail in Chapter 3.

2.3.1.2 Sequence identification from experimental data

It is an important bioinformatics problem to determine the biological sequences such as DNA sequences and protein sequences from the data generated by wet lab experiments. Because of the significant differences among technologies and methods used for generating experimental data, the sequence identification problem has several variants that are totally different from the computational viewpoint. For the purpose of illustration, the identification problems for DNA sequences and protein sequences are briefly discussed.

DNA sequence identification from DNA sequencing data: To identify DNA sequences, the so-called DNA sequencing technology is widely used. In DNA

-	A	G	G	C	T	A	T	C	A	C	C	T	G
T	A	G	-	C	T	A	C	C	A	-	-	-	G
C	A	G	-	C	T	A	C	C	A	-	-	-	G
C	A	G	-	C	T	A	T	C	A	C	-	G	G
C	A	G	-	C	T	A	T	C	G	C	-	G	G

Figure 2.1 An example of the alignment of five biological sequences. Here "–" denotes the gap inserted between different residues.

sequencing, many copies of original DNA sequence are cut into millions of fragments. Each copy is cut in a different way, so a fragment from one copy may overlap fragments from another. Given a set of fragments, the sequence assembly is to align and merge fragments to reconstruct the original DNA sequence.

Protein sequence identification from mass spectrometry data: In the identification of protein sequences, a protein is first digested into peptides by proteases such as trypsin. Then, the tandem mass spectrometer breaks peptides into even smaller fragments and records the mass of each fragment in a mass spectrum. The peptide sequence identification problem is to derive the sequence of a peptide given its mass spectrum. The identified peptide sequences are further assembled to infer protein sequences in the so-called protein inference procedure. The problem of protein inference is discussed in Chapter 5.

2.3.1.3 Sequence classification and regression

Many problems in biology require the accurate prediction of certain properties of biological sequences. For instance, the primary DNA sequence is highly correlated with the functional and structural protein properties. However, such relationships are still not fully understood. Therefore, computational prediction methods have to be used for advancing our understanding. Likewise, the accurate prediction of candidate PTM sites is of crucial importance for reducing the cost and time of wet lab validation. Overall, all of these bioinformatics problems can be essentially modeled as a sequence classification or regression problem. Here two representative bioinformatics applications are used for illustration purposes.

Sequence classification for phosphorylation site prediction: Phosphorylation is one of the most important and widely studied PTM events. The experimental determination of phosphorylation sites by wet labs is time consuming and labor intensive. Alternatively, one feasible approach is to collect a set of known phosphorylated peptides and another set of unphosphorylated peptides to construct a training data set. Based on the training data, a classification model is built from the labeled peptide sequences for predicting unknown phosphorylation events. The phosphorylation site prediction problem is presented in detail in Chapter 4.

Sequence regression for peak intensity prediction: Mass spectrometry is an important technique in proteomics for analyzing complex protein samples. To perform accurate protein quantification, one key problem is to predict peak intensities from peptide sequences. This is actually a sequence regression problem.

2.3.2 Structures

Structural biology is a branch of molecular biology, which is mainly concerned with the "tertiary structure" of biological macromolecules and complexes. The tertiary structure of a macromolecule is its three-dimensional structure. Macromolecules carry out most of the functions of cells on the basis of precise tertiary structures. Therefore, many bioinformatics researches focus on the study of tertiary structures of macromolecules such as RNA and proteins. Similar to the sequence-central research, bioinformatics problems with respect to tertiary structures of macromolecules can be divided into three different classes: (1) *multiple structure analysis*, (2) *structure prediction*, and (3) *structure-based prediction*.

2.3.2.1 Multiple structure analysis

The comparison of multiple structures and the discovery of common patterns from a set of structures have numerous applications in life science. Protein structure patterns can be used for characterizing families of proteins that are functionally or structurally related. Such patterns can reveal the relationships between sequences, structures, and functions of proteins. Two representative bioinformatics problems in this category are structural alignment and structural motif discovery.

Structural alignment: The goal of structural alignment is to establish the homology between two or more structures based on their three-dimensional conformation. This procedure is usually applied to protein tertiary structures, which can transfer information about a well-known protein to unknown proteins that can be structurally aligned to it.

Structural motif discovery: One structural motif is a recurring set of residues spatially close in three dimensions, but not necessarily adjacent in the sequence. Such motifs are useful for revealing interesting evolutionary and functional relationships among proteins when the sequence similarity between proteins is very low.

2.3.2.2 Structure prediction

Due to the limitation of instruments and technologies, it is still very difficult to obtain the tertiary structure of every RNA and protein through wet lab experiments. Therefore, the computational prediction of the three-dimensional structure of a protein or RNA from its primary sequence is a complementary approach for biologists. Taking the protein structure prediction as an example, a large number of prediction tools have been developed during the past 20 years. These tools adopt different principles such as homology modeling, protein threading, and *ab initio* methods.

2.3.2.3 Structure-based prediction

The structure information is the main determinant of functions in a cell. Therefore, the three-dimensional information of proteins is critical to many bioinformatics applications, such as the prediction of protein–protein interactions (PPIs), protein functions, and drug targets. This family of bioinformatics problems can be unified under the umbrella of "structure-based prediction."

2.3.3 Networks

Complex biological systems are generally represented and analyzed as networks, where vertices represent biological units and edges represent the interactions between the units. The different types of biological networks include gene regulatory networks, gene coexpression networks, metabolic networks, signaling networks, PPI networks, and more. The large number of network-related bioinformatics problems can be categorized into several classes: (1) *network analysis*, (2) *network inference*, and (3) *network-assisted prediction*.

2.3.3.1   Network analysis

To gain insight into the organization and structure of the large biological networks, various topological structures and properties, dynamic properties, and functionality–topology relationships are expected to be addressed by the analysis of networks. Network analysis is becoming the key methodology for studying complex biological systems. There are many biological network analysis tasks. Here the *network comparison* problem is used as a representative network analysis problem.

Network comparison: This is the process of contrasting two or more biological networks from different species, conditions, or interaction types. If the target networks are PPI networks, many fundamental biological questions at the protein level can be addressed. For instance, the comparison results may tell which protein interactions are likely to have equivalent functions across species. Furthermore, it is also possible to reveal the underlying evolution of proteins, networks, and even the whole species.

Generally, three types of computational methods are available for network comparison: network alignment, network integration, and network querying. Network alignment identifies regions of similarity by globally comparing two networks, which is typically applied to detect subnetworks that are conserved across species. Network integration is to integrate networks of different types from the same species to gain a more comprehensive understanding on the overall biological system under study. The integration is achieved by merging different network types into a single network with multiple types of interactions over the same set of elements. Network querying searches a network to find subnetworks that are similar to a given subnetwork.

2.3.3.2   Network inference

It is often impossible or expensive to determine the network structure by experimental validation of all interaction pairs between biological units. A more practical approach is to infer the network structure from the indirect evidence hidden in the biological experimental data. Network inference is the process of making inferences and predictions about underlying network by analyzing the experimental data.

The topic of biological network inference is of great interest and has been extensively investigated. There are many methods for inferring different types of biological networks such as gene regulatory networks and PPI networks. For example, the combination of affinity purification with mass spectrometry analysis has become one of the leading methods for PPI network construction. To derive the underlying network structure between proteins, many computational methods have been developed, which we present in Chapters 6 and 7.

2.3.3.3   Network-assisted prediction

The available large-scale networks of molecular interactions within the cell make it possible to study many bioinformatics problems in the context of a network. Typical applications include the prediction of protein functions, disease genes, and drug–target interactions. The basic idea of such network-assisted prediction is to use the correlation information between biological entities in the network to improve the prediction accuracy.

2.4 Challenges in biological data mining

With the development of life sciences, large-scale biological data sets are generated at various levels: genome, transcriptome, epigenome, proteome, metabolome, molecular imaging, different population of people, and clinical records. To analyze these large amounts of biological data, new bioinformatics tools and techniques should be developed to overcome many challenges.

Due to the complexity of biological systems and current limitations of instruments, the majority of biological data sets are quite noisy and highly complicated. Therefore, the development of effective data preprocessing methods is critical to the success of biological data analysis.

Data mining probably is the most popular computational tool in molecular biology. Many bioinformatics problems can be cast as standard data mining problems so that existing methods can be applied. However, some bioinformatics problems cannot be modeled as existing data mining tasks, making it necessary to develop new data mining techniques and solutions.

In addition, it is still very challenging to provide sustained performance estimates for some bioinformatics algorithms. This problem will become more serious when there are no benchmark data sets or the underlying ground truth is still lacking. For example, the entire PPI networks for most species are still not established, making it difficult to accurately evaluate the performance of PPI network inference algorithms. Therefore, more research should be devoted to the development of effective validation algorithms for assessing the data mining results in bioinformatics applications.

2.5 Summary

Bioinformatics is a field that is still advancing rapidly, making it impossible to cover all the contents of bioinformatics even within a book. In this chapter, some bioinformatics and related data analysis tasks are introduced. For further reading, I would like to recommend two popular bioinformatics textbooks [2,3].

References

[1] X. Huang, et al., No-boundary thinking in bioinformatics research, BioData Min. 6 (2013) 19.
[2] N.C. Jones, P. Pevzner, An Introduction to Bioinformatics Algorithms, MIT Press, Cambridge, MA, 2004.
[3] J.M. Claverie, C. Notredame, Bioinformatics for Dummies, John Wiley & Sons, New York, 2011.

Phosphorylation motif discovery

3

3.1 Background and problem description

Posttranslational modification (PTM) is the chemical modification of a protein after its translation. Protein phosphorylation is one special kind of PTM that plays important roles in many cellular processes. Generally, phosphorylation can only happen on three docking sites: serine (S), threonine (T), and tyrosine (Y). A biological function usually involves a series of phosphorylation processes, in which protein kinases recognize specific protein substrates.

The advances in high-throughput techniques such as the tandem mass spectrometry make it possible to rapidly and directly recognize large-scale phosphorylation sites in a single experiment. Such sets of identified phosphopeptides provide valuable information for determining the specific kinase–substrate recognition.

Phosphorylation motifs are consensus amino acids that are aligned upstream and downstream of the phosphorylation sites. The discovery of phosphorylation motifs is to detect a set of motifs that occur more frequently in the set of phosphorylated peptides P (i.e., the foreground data) than that in the set of unphosphorylated peptides N (i.e., the background data). In other words, the identified phosphorylation motifs are all "over-expressed" in P. The phosphorylation motifs not only provide information about the specificities of the kinases involved, but also reveal the underlying regulation mechanism and facilitate the prediction of unknown phosphorylation sites.

One phosphorylation motif can be represented as a string with a single phosphorylated residue that is denoted with an underlined character, for example, S̲, T̲, or Y̲. The string representation of motifs consists of either conserved positions or wild positions (denoted by "."). For instance, "PS̲.D" is a phosphorylation motif that has two conserved positions. These two fixed residues on the conserved positions are "P" (one position on the left) and "D" (two positions on the right), respectively.

One motif A is said to be a k-motif if it has k conserved positions. If another motif B contains only a subset of these k amino acids at the corresponding positions in A, then B is called a submotif of A. For example, "PS̲.D" is a 2-motif and "S̲.D" is a 1-motif. In addition, "S̲.D" is a submotif of "PS̲.D."

Table 3.1 is a sample data set used for phosphorylation motif discovery. In this example, there are 10 phosphorylated peptides in the foreground data P and 10 unphosphorylated peptides in the background data N, respectively. Each peptide has 13 amino acids and its central position is the phosphorylation site. In this example data set, we can observe that "KMS̲" is an interesting phosphorylation motif because it appears five times in P but never occurs in N. In contrast, "K.S̲" is not a meaningful phosphorylation motif because its appearance frequencies in P and N are equal.

Data Mining for Bioinformatics Applications. http://dx.doi.org/10.1016/B978-0-08-100100-4.00003-X

Table 3.1 **A sample data set used for phosphorylation motif discovery**

Foreground data P	Background data N
GLKLKMSMQYPEG	EACPKHSWHTAHY
VLAYKMSWDPEVR	RGASKGSMVRFKG
QDPAKMSMQLATE	RQAVKPSWVARKY
LPYMKMSWLCSLA	LGVQKRSKHDRAH
HPGEKMSGALQDA	HVGAKRSADCANS
SWDTQASKTRDAL	DKHSQMSVRSQND
AKLQGWSTVTRGS	VCQADMSAVQRYS
VKQLAWSPVKMTS	SPWDTMSDYSDLQ
NLYWQTSEVLWRV	QKLQPMSPALLQG
HASDWPSEQPKMP	DPQHLMSRQEALG

Both the foreground data set and background data set consist of 10 peptide sequences, where the length of each peptide sequence is 13. The underlined central residue is the phosphorylation site.

3.2   The nature of the problem

If we consider the phosphorylation state as the class feature, the data sets used in phosphorylation motif discovery can be divided into two classes. Essentially, the problem of phosphorylation motif discovery can be modeled as a special discriminative pattern mining problem in the literature of data mining. More precisely, three mapping relationships between these two tasks can be observed.

First, by taking the position-specific amino acid set as the collection of all possible feature values, the peptide sequences in phosphorylation motif discovery correspond to the samples in discriminative pattern mining. Second, the phosphorylation motifs can be considered as the target patterns when mining discriminative patterns from class-labeled data sets. Last, the over-expression level of phosphorylation motifs can be calculated by statistical measures used for assessing the power of discriminative patterns.

Therefore, the task of phosphorylation motif discovery can be referred to as an example of discriminative pattern mining.

3.3   Data collection

To conduct the phosphorylation motif discovery, we first need to collect phosphorylation sites that have been experimentally verified. There are already more than 20 phosphorylation-related databases that store known phosphorylation sites.[1] Typically, these databases focus on phosphorylation sites of certain organisms. For instance, the PhosPhAt database is designed specifically to store and query Arabidopsis phosphorylation sites.

---

[1]In Ref. [1], some of the most popular phosphorylation-related databases are listed with sufficient details.

These verified phosphorylation sites in the databases are used for constructing the foreground data P. We also need to collect data that can be used to generate the background data N, which are peptides that cannot be phosphorylated. Hence, the entire protein sequence database of the target organisms or species should be collected as well in this phase.

3.4 Data preprocessing

Before conducting the discovery procedure for finding phosphorylation motifs, the raw data from the phosphorylation site database and the protein sequence database should be preprocessed to generate the tabular formed data. The typical preprocessing process works as follows:

- The peptides in the phosphorylation site database are first mapped back to their prospective proteins. Then, a fixed number of residues upstream and downstream of the phosphorylation site are reextracted from the protein sequences. Here the number of residues r is usually not large, for example, $r = 10$. This procedure guarantees that we can obtain the foreground data P with a fixed number of features.
- To generate the background data set N, the peptides of length $2r + 1$ with a phosphorylated residue in the center position are extracted from the corresponding protein database. Then, all peptides already in P are removed. Finally, a desired fraction of peptides are sampled from the remaining peptides to form the background data.

3.5 Modeling: A discriminative pattern mining perspective

The problem of phosphorylation motif discovery has been widely studied, and several effective algorithms have been proposed based on discriminative pattern mining techniques. On the one hand, some methods employ the exhaustive strategy and some approaches adopt the heuristic strategy to discover as many significant motifs as possible. On the other hand, some methods apply the frequency test to mine a set of frequent motifs as candidates first, and then employ the statistical significance evaluation to obtain significant motifs by filtering out insignificant ones, whereas other methods conduct these two assessments in a single stage to directly generate the significant motifs. The approaches proposed in Refs. [2,3] are two representative ones, which tackle the problem of mining phosphorylation motifs from the viewpoint of mining discriminative patterns. Here we will use the Motif-All algorithm [2] and the C-Motif algorithm [3] as examples to show how the discriminative pattern mining methods can be used to solve the problem of phosphorylation motif discovery.

3.5.1 The Motif-All algorithm

The Motif-All algorithm takes the support threshold and the significance threshold as input to find phosphorylation motifs from the set of phosphorylated peptides P and the set of unphosphorylated peptides N. As shown in Figure 3.1, this algorithm has the following steps:

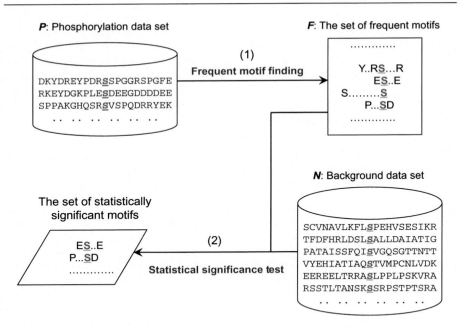

Figure 3.1 Overview of the Motif-All algorithm. In the first phase, it finds frequent motifs from *P* to reduce the number of candidate motifs. In the second phase, it performs the significance testing procedure to report all statistically significant motifs to the user.

1. Finding the set of all frequent motifs *F* from *P* using frequent pattern mining algorithms such as the Apriori algorithm [4]. A motif is said to be frequent if its support value (frequency) in *P* is no less than a user-specified support threshold.
2. Scanning the background set *N* to calculate the statistical significance for each motif in *F*. Those motifs that can pass the significance threshold are reported to the user. Popular measures such as the odds ratio and the risk ratio can be used for evaluating the statistical significance of motifs. The use of alternative significance measures will not change the nature of the problem and affect the property of the algorithm.

The Motif-All algorithm adopts the popular two-stage strategy used in discriminative pattern mining for phosphorylation motif discovery. This method is simple and effective. However, it evaluates the statistical significance of each motif without considering the effect of its subsets, making it possible to generate many redundant motifs whose over-expressiveness mainly comes from their submotifs. To alleviate this issue, the C-Motif algorithm [3] not only evaluates the statistical significance of each motif but also presents another measure called conditional significance to remove the effect of submotifs.

3.5.2 The C-Motif algorithm

C-Motif is implemented in a single stage where the frequency and the statistical significance values are tested at the same time, as shown in Figure 3.2. That is, this algorithm visits the candidate motifs in a breath-first manner. For each motif, the support,

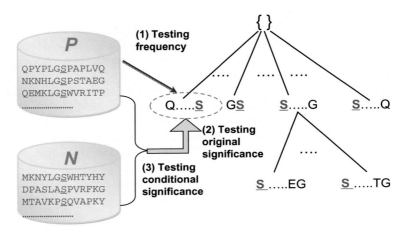

Figure 3.2 Overview of the C-Motif algorithm. The algorithm generates and tests candidate phosphorylation motifs in a breath-first manner, where the support and the statistical significance values are evaluated simultaneously.

the original statistical significance, and the conditional statistical significance are evaluated simultaneously. Here the original statistical significance is calculated over the data sets P and N. The calculation of conditional statistical significance is illustrated in Figure 3.3.

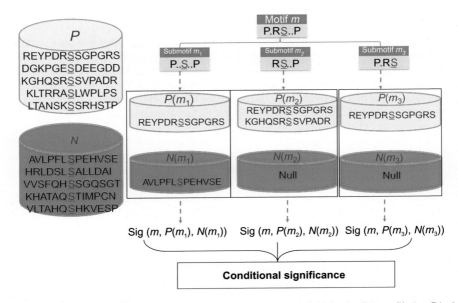

Figure 3.3 The calculation of conditional significance in C-Motif. In the figure, $Sig(m, P(m_i), N(m_i))$ denotes the new significance value of m on its ith submotif induced data sets.

Because the peptide that contains one target motif must also contain its submotifs, the set of peptides that contain this motif must be a subset of the collection of peptides that contain its submotif. In particular, there are exactly k submotifs of size $k-1$ for one k-motif. For each submotif of size $k-1$, we can generate a set of peptides in which every peptide contains this submotif.

As shown in Figure 3.3, the motif "P.RS..P" is a 3-motif and has three submotifs of size two. Each submotif will induce a new foreground data set and a new background data set by selecting peptides that contain the corresponding submotif. On each submotif induced data set, the statistical significance of the motif "P.RS..P" is recalculated. The conditional significance of "P.RS..P" is obtained by aggregating the three new significance values.

The use of conditional significance is able to remove the effect of submotifs. As a result, more redundant motifs are filtered out by C-Motif.

3.6   Validation: Permutation *p*-value calculation

Although methods such as C-Motif can reduce the number of reported phosphorylation motifs significantly, the validation of discovered motifs is still a nontrivial issue. This is because no multiple testing corrections are carried out in most phosphorylation motif discovery algorithms, leading to an inaccurate motif significance assessment. As a result, there are still some false positives in the returned motifs.

In order to assess the significance of phosphorylation motifs more accurately, the permutation test is generally used to calculate the empirical p-value of each motif. The standard permutation procedure works as follows:

1. Formulate a permutation null hypothesis and choose a test statistic that will have different values under the null hypothesis and the alternative hypothesis. Here the null hypothesis is that the frequencies of motifs in foreground data and background data are the same. And the alternative hypothesis is that the frequency distributions of motifs in the foreground data and the background data are different. Furthermore, the choice of test statistic is flexible because one can use any statistical significance measures that are appropriate for evaluating the over-expressiveness of phosphorylation motifs.
2. Permute class labels (phosphorylated vs. unphosphorylated) in a way that is consistent with the null hypothesis of the test and the study designed to produce permuted data sets, then calculate the test statistic values of all tested motifs in these permuted data sets to generate the null distribution.
3. Calculate the original test statistic values of all tested motifs in the original data set. The p-values of all phosphorylation motifs can be calculated by locating the original test statistic values in the null distribution.

To illustrate the permutation procedure, one example is shown in Table 3.2. In this sample data set, there are two phosphorylated peptides and four unphosphorylated peptides whose class labels are denoted by "T" and "F," respectively. Table 3.3 shows one possible permuted data set after random permutation. That is, the new foreground

Table 3.2 **The original foreground data P and the background data N before the permutation**

Number	Peptide sequence	Class
1	DGYDRRYGDRYSPGGRSPGFE	T
2	DGNEVVEPVDYGKSKADDEFE	T
3	AEKKKTKKPSYPSSSMKSKVY	F
4	MTKDELTEEEYLSGKDYLDPP	F
5	RHKDSLAAAEYPDGMKVSNSH	F
6	GGTAVGKDLLYDGDSVKSSTD	F

In this example, there are two peptides in P and four peptides in N.

Table 3.3 **One example randomized data set after permutation**

Number	Peptide sequence	Class
1	DGYDRRYGDRYSPGGRSPGFE	F
2	DGNEVVEPVDYGKSKADDEFE	F
3	AEKKKTKKPSYPSSSMKSKVY	F
4	MTKDELTEEEYLSGKDYLDPP	T
5	RHKDSLAAAEYPDGMKVSNSH	T
6	GGTAVGKDLLYDGDSVKSSTD	F

data in the randomized data set are composed of the fourth peptide and fifth peptide instead of the first two peptides.

The standard permutation method is simple to implement and provides empirical p-values for motifs in which we are interested. However, the p-values for the motifs of different sizes are tested together in the standard permutation. That is, all motifs use the same permutation null.

Because the number of possible motifs increases rapidly with their sizes and motifs of the larger sizes are prone to have small p-values, the motifs of smaller size may be overwhelmed if we use the same permutation null. This problem will become increasingly serious as the size of motifs under investigation increases.

To overcome this limitation, Ref. [5] adopts a new permutation method that tests motifs of different sizes separately with different permutation nulls. The basic idea is to first test 1-motifs in the same manner as that in the standard permutation. In testing 2-motifs, the effects detected in the 1-motifs are incorporated into the construction of null distribution. Similarly, the effects detected in 1-motifs and 2-motifs are considered when testing the 3-motifs. This procedure continues until there are no frequent motifs with larger size that can be found for the significance testing.

3.7   Discussion and future perspective

Since the problem of phosphorylation motif discovery was introduced in 2005 by Schwartz and Gygi [6], many algorithms have been proposed from different angles [2,3,7–9]. Although some of these methods are designed regardless of the fact that the phosphorylation motif discovery problem is a discriminative pattern mining problem in essence, their key ideas have similar counterparts in the literature of discriminative pattern mining [10]. Hence, the advances in discriminative pattern mining will promote the development of more effective phosphorylation motif mining methods.

Despite the algorithmic advances in phosphorylation motif discovery, several challenging problems are still unsolved. To follow is a list of interesting and challenging problems that should be further investigated in the future.

First, although methods such as C-Motif can reduce the number of phosphorylation motifs, there are still many redundant or meaningless phosphorylation motifs that are reported to the users. Hence, it is necessary to develop more effective algorithms for further improving the precision of returned motifs. In particular, it is desirable to have a statistically sound significance measure that is able to remove the effect of submotifs in a natural manner.

Second, existing algorithms merely use the sequence data around the phosphorylation sites to conduct the analysis. This may prevent us from finding really biologically relevant patterns to derive useful scientific discoveries. To overcome this limitation, it is plausible to conduct motif search on expanded data sets that include additional features such as the three-dimensional protein structures.

Third, the construction of foreground data and background data in the literature is based on the direct extraction of a certain number of amino acids around a phosphorylation site. These amino acids from different peptides are aligned in a very rude manner. Indeed, it is highly necessary to perform sequence alignment with multiple sequence alignment algorithms before the motif extraction procedure. The challenge here is how to align thousands of short sequences rapidly and accurately.

Fourth, the permutation test procedure for testing the statistical significance of phosphorylation motifs has demonstrated its effectiveness in practice. However, there are several disadvantages in the direct permutation method. One is the p-values of a same motif may be inconsistent in different runs due to the effect of random sampling. Additionally, the computational cost of permutation-based method is very high. To obtain more accurate and stable results, more permutations have to be generated, rendering a more time-consuming task. These disadvantages limit the usability of the permutation-based method. Clearly, these disadvantages are caused by the inexact null distributions, that is, the null distribution generated in each run is only an approximate one. As a result, the permutation p-values of phosphorylation motifs calculated from it are also not exact. Hence, the algorithms that can generate an exact null distribution should be developed so as to obtain exact empirical p-values for accurately assessing the statistical significance of phosphorylation motifs.

Finally, the performance comparison of different algorithms is still not fully solved due to the lack of public benchmark data sets. In this regard, an alternative choice is to generate simulated data with known ground truth. However, there is still no widely accepted simulation procedure for producing such synthetic data for performance evaluation. Thus, it is highly necessary to design a good simulator for this purpose.

References

[1] Y. Xue, et al., A summary of computational resources for protein phosphorylation, Curr. Protein Pept. Sci. 11 (2010) 485–496.

[2] Z. He, C. Yang, G. Guo, et al., Motif-all: discovering all phosphorylation motifs, BMC Bioinf. 12 (Suppl. 1) (2011) S22.

[3] X. Liu, J. Wu, H. Gong, et al., Mining conditional phosphorylation motifs, IEEE/ACM Trans. Comput. Biol. Bioinform. 11 (5) (2014) 915–927.

[4] R. Agrawal, R. Srikant, Fast algorithms for mining association rules, in: Proceedings of the 20th International Conference on Very Large Data Bases, 1994, pp. 487–499.

[5] H. Gong, Z. He, Permutation methods for testing the significance of phosphorylation motifs, Stat. Interface 5 (1) (2012) 61–73.

[6] D. Schwartz, S.P. Gygi, An iterative statistical approach to the identification of protein phosphorylation motifs from large scale data sets, Nat. Biotechnol. 23 (11) (2005) 1391–1398.

[7] A. Ritz, G. Shakhnarovich, A.R. Salomon, B.J. Raphael, Discovery of phosphorylation motif mixtures in phosphoproteomics data, Bioinformatics 25 (1) (2009) 14–21.

[8] Y.-C. Chen, et al., Discovery of protein phosphorylation motifs through exploratory data analysis, PLoS One 6 (5) (2011) e20025.

[9] T. Wang, et al., MMFPh: a maximal motif finder for phosphoproteomics datasets, Bioinformatics 28 (12) (2012) 1562–1570.

[10] X. Liu, J. Wu, F. Gu, et al., Discriminative pattern mining and its applications in bioinformatics. Brief. Bioinform (2015). http://dx.doi.org/10.1093/bib/bbu042.

Phosphorylation site prediction

4

4.1 Background and problem description

In an eukaryotic cell, it is estimated that about 30–50% of the proteins can be phosphorylated. In recent years, high-throughput studies have been able to identify new phosphorylation sites rapidly. Unfortunately, biological methods for phosphorylation event recognition are still costly and time consuming. In particular, the mass spectrometry-based techniques are biased toward abundant proteins and are difficult to provide specific information regarding the protein kinase–substrate interactions. Hence, the computational prediction method is potentially a useful alternative strategy for annotating the phosphorylation sites on the whole proteome scale.

Most proposed computational methods formulate the problem of phosphorylation site prediction as a binary classification problem, in which the class feature is the phosphorylation status. Although amino acids such as histidine and aspartate can also be phosphorylated, only serine (S), threonine (T), and tyrosine (Y) are considered frequently in most computational models.

4.2 Data collection and data preprocessing

As discussed in Chapter 3, we need to collect both the database of known phosphorylation sites and the corresponding protein sequence database to construct the data sets used for data analysis.

Fundamental to any classification problem, it is critical to generate training data and testing data for model construction and performance evaluation. In the context of binary classification, both the training data and testing data have two classes: positive data and negative data. Here, positive data contain a set of phosphorylated peptides, and negative data consist of a set of nonphosphorylated peptides. However, it is nontrivial to generate such kinds of data due to the uncertainty of phosphorylation events and the existence of unrecognized phosphorylation sites. As a result, different strategies have been proposed to construct the training/testing data.

Reference [1] provides a summary on both training and testing data construction methods in the literature. The phosphorylation site prediction task can be further divided into two more specific prediction tasks: non-kinase-specific phosphorylation site prediction and kinase-specific phosphorylation site prediction. For these two subtasks, the data construction methods for training data and testing data are different as well.

4.2.1 Training data construction

Typical training data construction methods for non-kinase-specific phosphorylation site prediction are listed as follows:

1. *GTrainP*: The positive training data are composed of phosphorylated peptides that have been experimentally recognized.
2. *GTrainN1*: The negative training data contain only unphosphorylated peptides from phosphorylated proteins. One protein is called a phosphorylated protein if it has at least one S/T/Y residue that is known to be phosphorylated.
3. *GTrainN2*: The negative training data are composed of unphosphorylated peptides from both phosphorylated proteins and unphosphorylated proteins.
4. *GTrainN3*: The negative training data contain only unphosphorylated peptides from unphosphorylated proteins.
5. *GTrainN4*: This method first calculates the frequency distribution of amino acids of the peptides from GTrainN1. Then it randomly generates a set of new peptides according to the calculated frequency distribution as the negative training data.
6. *GTrainN5*: This method randomly generates a set of peptides with equal frequency distribution of amino acids as the negative training data.

To provide a vivid illustration, Figure 4.1 describes the constituent parts for the training data set generated from GTrainP, GTrainN1, GTrainN2, and GTrainN3.

The training data construction methods for kinase-specific phosphorylation site prediction are more diverse, as described below (see also Figure 4.2).

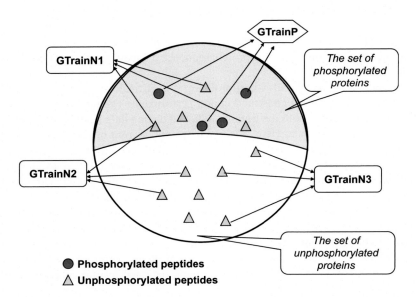

Figure 4.1 An illustration on the training data construction methods for non-kinase-specific phosphorylation site prediction. Here the shadowed part denotes the set of phosphorylated proteins and the unshadowed area represents the set of unphosphorylated proteins.

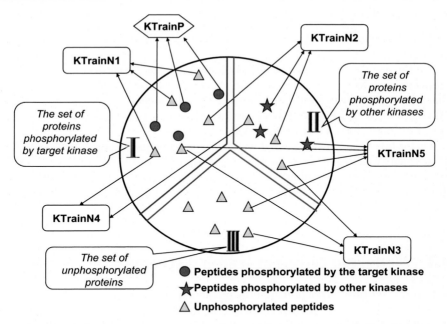

Figure 4.2 An illustration on the training data construction methods for kinase-specific phosphorylation site prediction. The proteins are divided into three parts: (**I**) the set of proteins that are phosphorylated by the target kinase, (**II**) the set of proteins that are phosphorylated by the other kinases, and (**III**) the set of unphosphorylated proteins.

1. *KTrainP*: The positive training data consist of verified phosphorylated peptides from phosphorylated proteins of the target kinase.
2. *KTrainN1*: The negative training data are composed of unphosphorylated peptides from phosphorylated proteins of the target kinase.
3. *KTrainN2*: The negative training data contain both unphosphorylated peptides from all phosphorylated proteins and those phosphorylated peptides from proteins that are not phosphorylated by the target kinase.
4. *KTrainN3*: The negative training data are constructed with unphosphorylated peptides from both phosphorylated proteins and unphosphorylated proteins.
5. *KTrainN4*: The negative training data are composed of unphosphorylated peptides from proteins that can be phosphorylated by any kinase.
6. *KTrainN5*: The negative training data include both unphosphorylated peptides from all proteins and phosphorylated peptides from proteins phosphorylated by other kinases.
7. *KTrainN6*: The negative training set are composed of unphosphorylated peptides whose phosphorylation residues are buried in the core of proteins phosphorylated by the target kinase. This method assumes that buried residues would not be physically accessible to any kinase, thus improving the quality of negative training data.

For both non-kinase-specific and kinase-specific predictions, the empirical comparison shows that different training data construction methods have different prediction performance and the difference is significant according to several statistical tests [1].

4.2.2   Feature extraction

To generate features for classifier training and testing, there are two widely adopted strategies in the literature.

On the one hand, one may directly view the data as a categorical data, where the amino acids at each position correspond to categorical feature values. For classifiers that cannot handle categorical data, each categorical feature can be transformed into 20 binary features, where each binary feature represents the presence or absence of a specific amino acid on that position with 1/0.

On the other hand, many methods extract some predefined features artificially. The most widely used features are the sequence compositions of amino acids surrounding phosphorylation sites. In addition, other more complex features are often adopted in different methods, such as the protein disorder features and features related with spatial amino acid compositions.

4.3   Modeling: Different learning schemes

In Ref. [2], existing phosphorylation site prediction tools are summarized and categorized from different viewpoints. These techniques differ in several ways: the machine learning or data mining techniques used; the features extracted from the set of peptides; whether predictions are kinase-specific or non-kinase-specific; and the construction of training and testing data.

Here we discuss the key modeling part from a different angle: the taxonomy of underlying machine learning principles.

4.3.1   Standard supervised learning

Almost all the existing prediction tools for phosphorylation sites fall into this category. That is, a classifier is first built from the given training data and then applied to predicting the class label of S/T/Y residues whose property is unknown. With respect to the classifier used, the most popular technique is support vector machine (SVM), which is exploited in many prediction tools (e.g., Musite [3]).

4.3.2   Active learning

Those tools based on supervised learning have been successfully applied to many organisms for phosphorylation site prediction. However, there is useful information inherent within the set of nonannotated S/T/Y sites that could be exploited for building more accurate classifiers. It is well-known that the number of nonannotated S/T/Y sites is much larger than the number of annotated ones.

To fully use the information in the S/T/Y sites whose phosphorylation status is still unknown, Ref. [4] presents an active learning strategy to train classifiers for phosphorylation site prediction.

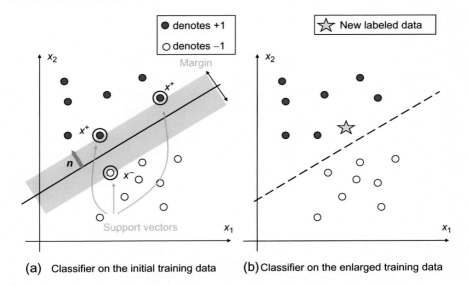

(a) Classifier on the initial training data   (b) Classifier on the enlarged training data

Figure 4.3 An illustration on the basic idea of the active learning procedure for phosphorylation site prediction. (a) The SVM classifier (solid line) generated from the original training data. (b) The new SVM classifier (dashed line) built from the enlarged training data. The enlarged training data are composed of the initial training data and a new labeled sample.

As shown in Figure 4.3a, an SVM classifier (solid line) is first built on the initial training data, where solid circles represents phosphorylated peptides (+1) and the empty circle denotes the unphosphorylated peptides (−1). The classifier is applied to evaluating a set of unlabeled peptides and the peptide with the highest classification confidence is marked with its new label. Then, this marked peptide, which is represented as a star in Figure 4.3b, is added into the training data set to generate a new enlarged training data set. On this new training data set, a new SVM classifier (dashed line) is learned. This update procedure is repeated until some stopping criteria are satisfied, for example, a sufficient number of new samples have been included in the augmented training data.

4.3.3 Transfer learning

In the context of standard supervised learning, it is assumed that the training data and future testing data come from the same feature space, that is, have the same distribution. However, in the application of phosphorylation site prediction, the lack of sufficient training data with respect to experimentally confirmed phosphorylation sites hampers the development of more accurate prediction models.

To alleviate this issue, a novel prediction method called PHOSFER for applying phosphorylation data from other organisms to enhance the accuracy of predictions in a target organism is presented in Ref. [5]. Essentially, this approach falls into the so-called transfer learning framework [6]. Transfer learning is helpful in case we have a classification task in one domain of interest, but we only have sufficient training data in another domain of interest, where the latter may have a different data distribution [6]. In such cases, it would greatly improve the prediction performance if the knowledge in one domain can be transferred to the target domain successfully.

PHOSFER is a phosphorylation site prediction tool designed for organisms such as plants for which little phosphorylation site data are available. The soybean (Glycine max) is used as a test case to illustrate its feasibility and advantage. Basically, this method has the following steps, as described in Figure 4.4.

First of all, phosphorylation sites of nine different organisms that have been exper-imentally characterized are gathered from the corresponding online databases. In addition, the Basic Local Alignment Search Tool (BLAST) searches are used to deter-mine the degree of conservation between phosphorylation sites in soybean and those in other organisms.

Then, the known phosphorylation sites from both soybean and other organisms are used as the training data. Each training peptide from other organisms is assigned a weight based on the degree of phosphorylation site conservation between soybean and the corresponding organism and the number of training peptides from that organ-ism. The weights of training peptides from different organisms are determined accord-ing to the following principle: higher weights are given to peptides that are better conserved in soybean and from organisms with less known phosphorylation sites.

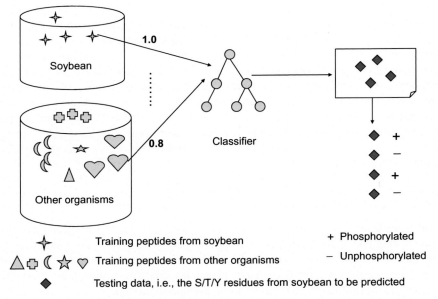

Figure 4.4 An overview of the PHOSFER method. The training data are constructed with peptides from both soybean and other organisms, in which different training peptides have different weights. The classifier (e.g., random forest) is built on the training data set to predict the phosphorylation status of remaining S/T/Y residues in the soybean organism.

Finally, the random forest classifier is generated on the weighted training data set collected from different organisms to predict the phosphorylation status of candidate S/T/Y residues in soybean. It has been demonstrated that the resultant predictor outperforms both the Arabidopsis-specific tools and a simpler machine-learning technique that uses only known phosphorylation sites from soybean.

4.4 Validation: Cross-validation and independent test

Cross-validation and independent test are widely used for evaluating the classification performance in the context of both non-kinase-specific and kinase-specific phosphorylation site prediction.

Cross-validation divides the training data into several disjointed parts of approximately equal size. Each part is selected in turn as the testing data, whereas the remaining parts are used as the training data. The prediction model built on the training data is then applied to predicting the class labels of testing data. This process is repeated until all parts have been masked once, and then the prediction accuracies across all blinded tests are combined to give an overall performance estimate.

Different from cross-validation, an independent test uses a third-party data set as the testing data. In the context of phosphorylation site prediction, there are three commonly used strategies:

1. *ID1*: The testing data are composed of a set of phosphorylated peptides and unphosphorylated peptides, which are extracted from proteins of the same species but have no overlap with the training data.
2. *ID2*: The testing data are constructed by selecting peptides from other species.
3. *ID3*: The testing data are sampled from the same set of peptides that is used for generating the training data.

4.5 Discussion and future perspective

The problem of phosphorylation site prediction is a typical sequence classification problem: to build a prediction model from a set of training sequences and classify unknown sequences into different categories. Different from the classification problem on feature vectors, sequences do not have explicit features. As a result, the sequence classification is a more challenging task than the classification on feature vectors.

Generally, the sequence classification methods can be divided into three categories [7]: feature-based methods, distance-based methods, and model-based methods. The feature-based method transforms a sequence into a feature vector and then applies conventional classification methods. The distance-based method uses a distance function to measure the similarity between sequences and then classifies the test sequence according to its nearest neighbors in the training data. The model-based method is built on generative models, which assume that the sequences in one class are generated from an underlying probabilistic model.

Currently, most phosphorylation site prediction methods are feature-based approaches, which extract predefined features from both the phosphorylated peptides and unphosphorylated peptides for constructing the predictive model. Because the classification performance is highly dependent on the chosen set of features, existing prediction tools have adopted different kinds of features in their methods. Even with sophisticated feature extraction approaches, the true relevant features are still difficult to capture because the domain-specific insight is either incomplete or hard to translate into effective features. Therefore, an alternative strategy is to automate the process of constructing effective features for the sequence classification (e.g., Ref. [8]). To date, there are still no algorithms for phosphorylation site prediction that are constructed with such automatic feature extraction strategies.

The distance-based methods and the model-based methods in sequence classification have not been widely used in phosphorylation site prediction. In the future, more research efforts should be devoted to these two categories with the goal that more accurate phosphorylation site prediction tools can be constructed.

On the other hand, the phosphorylation site prediction is largely modeled as a standard supervised learning problem. As presented in previous sections in this chapter, other learning schemes such as the active learning and the transfer learning have already been exploited to address this issue. Indeed, other learning schemes can be used to model the problem of phosphorylation site prediction as well. For instance, the transductive learning [9] is another choice, in which the samples that need to be predicted are already known in training the classifier. This learning scheme is particularly suitable to solve the phosphorylation site prediction problem because the samples that need to be predicted are those unknown S/T/Y sites in all the proteins across the whole proteome. Unfortunately, prediction tools based on this idea are still not available.

The cross-validation error estimation has been widely used in validation and performance comparison for phosphorylation site prediction. This procedure is "almost unbiased" when random sampling is used in fold generation. However, this is not true with separate sampling, where the positive data and negative data are independently sampled [10]. It has been shown that the classical cross-validation can have strong bias under the separate sampling in Ref. [10]. Therefore, to use cross-validation with separate sampling in phosphorylation site prediction in the future, one should use the separate-sampling version of cross-validation in Ref. [10] to avoid estimation bias in performance evaluation.

References

[1] H. Gong, X. Liu, J. Wu, Z. He, Data construction for phosphorylation site prediction, Brief. Bioinform. 15 (5) (2014) 839–855.
[2] B. Trost, A. Kusalik, Computational prediction of eukaryotic phosphorylation sites, Bioinformatics 27 (2011) 2927–2935.
[3] J. Gao, J. Thelen, A. Dunker, et al., Musite, a tool for global prediction of general and kinase-specific phosphorylation sites, Mol. Cell. Proteomics 9 (12) (2010) 2586–2600.
[4] J. Jiang, H. Ip, Active learning for the prediction of phosphorylation sites, in: D. Liu (Ed.), International Joint Conference on Neural Networks, 2008, pp. 3158–3165.

[5] B. Trost, A. Kusalik, Computational phosphorylation site prediction in plants using random forests and organism-specific instance weights, Bioinformatics 29 (6) (2013) 686–694.

[6] S. Pan, Q. Yang, A survey on transfer learning, IEEE Trans. Knowl. Data Eng. 22 (10) (2010) 1345–1359.

[7] Z. Xing, J. Pei, E.J. Keogh, A brief survey on sequence classification, SIGKDD Explor. 12 (1) (2010) 40–48.

[8] U. Kamath, K.D. Jong, A. Shehu, Effective automated feature construction and selection for classification of biological sequences, PLoS One 9 (7) (2014) e99982.

[9] V. Vapnik, Statistical Learning Theory, Wiley, New York, 1988.

[10] U.M. Braga-Neto, A. Zollanvari, E.R. Dougherty, Cross-validation under separate sampling: strong bias and how to correct it, Bioinformatics 30 (23) (2014) 3349–3355.

Protein inference in shotgun proteomics

5.1 Introduction to proteomics

Proteins are the key functional entities in the cell. Proteomics is the global analysis of proteins, which is critical to understanding how cells function. However, it is more challenging to gather information at the proteome level than at the genome and transcriptome levels [1]. This is because the proteome is complemented by alternative splicing and diverse posttranslational modifications. Meanwhile, proteins are interconnected with each other in the form of complexes and signaling networks that are highly divergent in time and space.

Mass spectrometry (MS) plays important roles in proteome analysis. With rapid developments in instrumentation, sample separation, and computational analysis, MS-based proteomics has been successfully used to characterize almost complete proteomes in a high-throughput manner [2]. Such maturation of MS-based proteomics will deliver answers to some important biological questions.

MS-based shotgun proteomics is a strategy that offers fast, high-throughput characterization of complex protein mixtures. In the experiments, the extracted proteins from the sample are first digested into peptides with protease such as trypsin. Enzymatic digestion of a full proteome can generate hundreds of thousands of peptides, making it unfeasible to perform the MS analysis directly. Hence, the liquid chromatography (LC) separation usually is first used to reduce the sample complexity before the MS analysis. Ideally, all peptides eluted from the LC should be captured by the mass spectrometer. However, this is not true since peptides compete for efficient ionization. Therefore, abundant peptides are more likely to be analyzed by the mass spectrometer than those less abundant peptides. As a result, not all peptides are captured by the mass spectrometer.

After ionization, peptide precursor ions are introduced into the mass spectrometer, which records both their mass-to-charge (m/z) ratio and intensity. The single-stage mass spectrum that is composed of peaks corresponding to peptide precursor ions is insufficient for ambiguous protein identification. Therefore, some single precursors are selected for further fragmentation to generate tandem mass spectra (MS/MS). In a tandem mass spectrum, there are generally two types of peaks: peaks generated from amino-terminal fragment ions ("b" ions) and peaks generated from carboxy-terminal fragment ions ("y" ions). The combination of precursor m/z and its tandem mass spectrum is used to determine peptide sequences, and then proteins are inferred from the identified peptides.

Finally, peptides and proteins are quantified (either relatively or absolutely) to generate protein abundance. These protein abundances are then interpreted and further used for biomarker discovery or protein–protein interaction network construction.

Data Mining for Bioinformatics Applications. http://dx.doi.org/10.1016/B978-0-08-100100-4.00005-3

5.2   Protein identification in proteomics

In shotgun proteomics, the computational procedure for protein identification has two main steps: peptide identification and protein inference. In peptide identification, we search the experimental tandem mass spectra against a protein sequence database to obtain a set of peptide-spectrum matches, or use the *de novo* sequencing to determine the peptide sequences without using the protein database. In protein inference, those identified peptides are assembled into a set of confident proteins. Figure 5.1 gives an illustration of the protein identification process. In this chapter, we focus on the protein inference problem.

5.3   Protein inference: Problem formulation

Computationally, the input for the protein inference problem is a bipartite graph: one set of nodes is composed of identified peptides and another set of nodes is composed of candidate proteins that have at least one constituent peptide [3]. The inference problem considered here is to find a subset of proteins that are actually present in the sample. To date, many computational approaches for protein inference have been proposed. The details of these existing methods and the challenges of protein inference problem are summarized and discussed in Ref. [4].

The protein inference problem has been investigated from different perspectives. For instance, Ref. [3] has recently formulated it as a linear programming problem. This chapter focuses on how to use data mining techniques to solve this problem and shows that it can be tackled with several different data mining formulations.

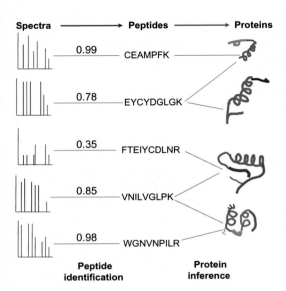

Figure 5.1 The protein identification process. In shotgun proteomics, the protein identification procedure has two main steps: peptide identification and protein inference.

5.4   Data collection

To infer proteins from identified peptides, the peptide identification results from the raw MS data and the corresponding protein sequence database should be collected. There are already several repositories of MS-derived proteomics data, such as PeptideAtlas (http://www.peptideatlas.org/) and PRIDE (http://www.ebi.ac.uk/pride/).

The PRIDE database offered by the European Bioinformatics Institute is one of the most prominent data repositories of MS-based proteomics data. The main data types stored in PRIDE are protein/peptide identifications, posttranslational modifications, raw mass spectra, and related metadata. As of September 2012, PRIDE contained 25,853 MS-based proteomics experiments, around 11.1 million identified proteins, 61.9 million identified peptides, and 324 million spectra.

5.5   Modeling with different data mining techniques

In this section, we use several different data mining techniques to solve the same protein inference problem. The analysis methods can be either supervised classification or unsupervised cluster analysis. This demonstrates that the same bioinformatics problem can be solved with fundamentally different data mining methods.

5.5.1   A classification approach

The BagReg method [5] formulates the protein inference problem as a standard supervised classification problem, which has three major phases: feature extraction, prediction model construction, and prediction result combination. Figure 5.2 gives an overview of this method.

In *feature extraction*, five features are generated from the original input data for each protein: the number of matched peptides, the number of unique peptides, the number of matched spectra, the maximal score of matched peptides, and the average score of matched peptides. As described in Figure 5.3, these five features are directly

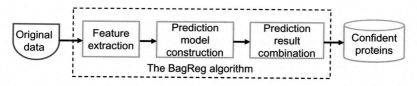

Figure 5.2 An overview of the BagReg method. It is composed of three major steps: feature extraction, prediction model construction, and prediction result combination. In feature extraction, the BagReg method generates five features that are highly correlated with the presence probabilities of proteins. In prediction model construction, five classification models are built and applied to predict the presence probability of proteins, respectively. In prediction result combination, the presence probabilities from different classification models are combined to obtain a consensus probability.

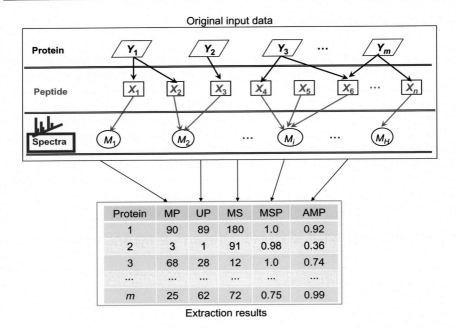

Figure 5.3 The feature extraction process. Five features are extracted from the original input data for each protein: the number of matched peptides (MP), the number of unique peptides (UP), the number of matched spectra (MS), the maximal score of matched peptides (MSP), and the average score of matched peptides (AMP).

obtained from the input data, and their values are numeric and easy to be calculated. Besides, there is a positive correlation between these feature values and the presence probabilities of proteins in the biological sample. That is, proteins with higher feature values are more likely to be present in the sample than those with lower feature values. This property brings much convenience to the construction of training data set.

In *prediction model construction*, several different learning models are generated independently. Because all five features are positively correlated with the presence probabilities of proteins, the training data set is constructed by taking each of the five features as the class feature. After that, classification methods are exploited to construct a predictive model on the training data and then the classification model is applied to predict presence probabilities for all proteins. Figure 5.4 gives an illustration of a single learning process.

In each single learning process, one feature is selected as the class feature and the other four features are regarded as dependent features. Because there is a positive correlation between the feature value and the protein presence possibility, the set of candidate proteins can be sorted based on the class feature value. Then, a portion of the top-ranked proteins is used as positive training set and a portion of proteins at the end of the sorted list is taken as the negative training set.

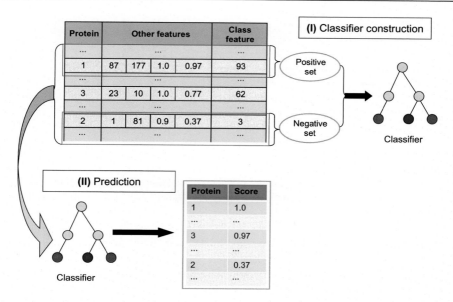

Figure 5.4 A single learning process. Each separate learning process accomplishes a typical supervised learning procedure. The model construction phase involves constructing the training set and learning the classification model. And the prediction phase is to predict the presence probabilities of all candidate proteins with the classifier obtained in the previous phase.

After the training set is generated, a learning model is ready to be built. Any classification model that could produce a probability as the prediction result can be applied. In BagReg, the logistic regression and Bayesian network are used to construct a predictive model on the training set and then predict the presence probabilities for all proteins.

In *prediction result combination*, the five scores of each protein are integrated to obtain a consensus score. The simplest method is to calculate the arithmetic mean of five scores.

5.5.2 A regression approach

The ProteinLasso method [6] formulates the protein inference problem as a constrained Lasso [7] regression problem. First, the probability of each identified peptide can be expressed as the linear combination of protein probabilities, where the coefficients are the conditional peptide probabilities given proteins. Such conditional peptide probabilities are called "peptide detectabilities," which is an intrinsic property of the peptide and can be predicted from existing identification results. Meanwhile, the probability of each identified peptide can be obtained from the peptide identification algorithm and some postprocessing methods.

If we take the protein probabilities as unknown variables and assume that peptide probabilities and peptide detectabilities are known in advance, the protein inference problem can be formulated as a constrained least squares regression problem. Here

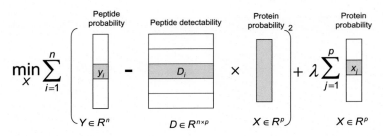

Figure 5.5 The basic idea of ProteinLasso. ProteinLasso formulates the protein inference problem as a minimization problem, where y_i is the peptide probability, D_i represents the vector of peptide detectabilities for the ith peptide, x_j denotes the unknown protein probability of the jth protein, and λ is a user-specified parameter. This optimization problem is the well-known Lasso regression problem in statistics and data mining.

some additional constraints are introduced as the probability of each protein should fall into [0, 1].

Furthermore, an additional penalty term is introduced into the model to make some variables to be zeros since the objective of protein inference is to find a subset of proteins that is truly present in the sample. Such modification leads to a constrained Lasso regression problem, as described in Figure 5.5.

5.5.3 A clustering approach

The protein inference problem can be modeled as a clustering problem as well, see Ref. [8]. Similar to the BagReg method, several different features for each protein can be extracted from the original input data, as shown in Figure 5.3. More precisely, the feature extraction procedure transforms the raw data into a tabular form, in which the columns represent features and rows correspond to proteins.

Although the class label (presence or absence) of each protein is unknown, the fact that these proteins can be divided into two groups is known in advance. One group is the set of proteins that really generates the identified peptides; another group is the set of proteins that is not present. Meanwhile, proteins in the same group have similar feature values. Based on the above observations, the clustering-based approach for protein inference is a two-step procedure: *cluster analysis* and *group identification*.

In the cluster analysis step, existing clustering algorithms such as k-means and hierarchical clustering are applied to partition the set of proteins into two clusters.

In the group identification step, the problem is to select one cluster as the set of truly present proteins. Because each feature is positively correlated with the protein presence probability, the cluster that has larger average feature values is selected.

5.6 Validation: Target-decoy versus decoy-free

How to assess the performance of different protein inference methods is a nontrivial problem. To date, there have already been some proteomics data sets in which the ground truth proteins are known in advance. However, such benchmark data sets

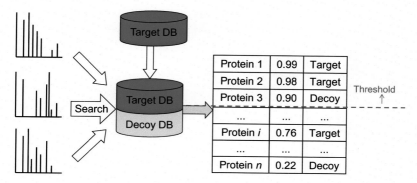

Figure 5.6 The target-decoy strategy for evaluating protein inference results. The MS/MS spectra are searched against the target-decoy database, and the identified proteins are sorted according to their scores or probabilities. The false discovery rate at a threshold can be estimated as the ratio of the number of decoy matches to that of target matches.

usually contain no more than 100 proteins, which cannot reflect the characteristics of real proteomics data sets.

5.6.1 Target-decoy method

The most popular approach for evaluating the identification results in the field of proteomics is the target-decoy strategy. As shown in Figure 5.6, the target-decoy strategy relies on a target-decoy database. This database contains all target protein sequences possibly present in the sample and an equal number of decoy sequences by reversing or reshuffling target protein sequences. During protein identification, the tandem mass spectra are searched against this target-decoy database. To validate the identification results, the false discovery rate (FDR) can be estimated as the ratio of the number of decoy matches to that of target matches.

The target-decoy approach is easy to understand and simple to implement. However, it has some drawbacks. First of all, searching both the target and the decoy database will double the running time of the protein identification procedure. In addition, the FDR estimation result can be unstable, as we usually use only one decoy database of the same size in the identification and evaluation process.

5.6.2 Decoy-free method

Different from the target-decoy approach, the decoy-free evaluation method estimates the FDR without searching the decoy database [9]. The decoy-free method in Ref. [9], as described in Figure 5.7, is based on the null hypothesis that each candidate protein matches an identified peptide totally at random. Under this null hypothesis, it first generates multiple random bipartite graphs with the same structure as the original one, that is, each protein (peptide) is connected to the same number of peptides (proteins).

To generate the null distribution, it is necessary to run the same protein inference method on these simulated graphs to obtain protein scores. However, it is time

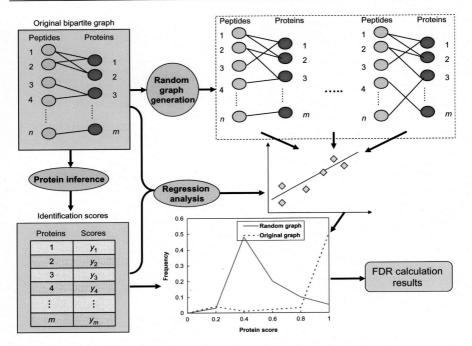

Figure 5.7 An overview of the decoy-free FDR estimation algorithm.

consuming and inconvenient to run some protein inference algorithms for many times. To alleviate this issue, a linear regression model is trained with the original bipartite graph and identification scores given by the target inference algorithm as the input. In this model, the class feature is the protein score, and the dependent features are peptide identification probabilities.

Then, the learned regression model is used as a substitute for the original protein inference method to predict protein scores on randomized graphs. If the null hypothesis that each protein matches an identified peptide by chance is true, then there is no significant difference between the score of each protein in the original graph and those calculated from the random graphs. Therefore, the permutation p-value of one protein can be calculated as the percentage of random graphs that produce a larger score than its score generated on the original graph. Based on these permutation p-values, the FDR at different cut-off thresholds can be derived according to some existing methods (e.g., Ref. [10]).

5.6.3   On unbiased performance evaluation for protein inference

Data mining is a cornerstone of modern bioinformatics. Meanwhile, an unbiased performance evaluation is undoubtedly the cornerstone of data mining research and applications, which provides a clear picture of the strengths and weaknesses of existing approaches.

In the real-world applications of data mining and machine learning methods, there are two closely related and separate problems: model selection and model assessment. In model selection, we estimate the performance of different models to choose the best one. In model assessment or performance evaluation, we test the prediction error of a final model obtained from the model selection process.

The protein inference problem is an instance of prediction task in data mining as well, as shown in Figure 5.8. In model selection, we use the peptide–protein bipartite graph as the input to find a "best" inference model that produces a vector $\bar{Y}$. Each element in $\bar{Y}$ can be either the probability/score that each protein is present or the presence status of each protein (true or false). In model assessment, we compare the predicted vector $\bar{Y}$ with ground truth vector Y to obtain the performance estimates. This is the correct procedure for evaluating and comparing protein inference algorithms.

In contrast, one possible mistake in an incorrect procedure is illustrated at the top of Figure 5.8: the partial or whole ground truth vector Y is used in the model selection process of protein inference algorithms. The problem is that the inference algorithms have an unfair advantage since they "have already seen" the absence/presence information in Y that should only be available during model assessment. In other words, the ground truth information has been leaked to the model selection phase. As a result, the performance estimates of inference algorithms will be overly optimistic. This phenomenon is essentially analogous to the selection bias observed in classification or regression due to feature selection over all samples prior to performance evaluation.

Such biased performance evaluation may occur when we use the target-decoy strategy for comparing the performance of different protein inference methods. In the target-decoy database search and evaluation strategy, a protein is regarded as a true

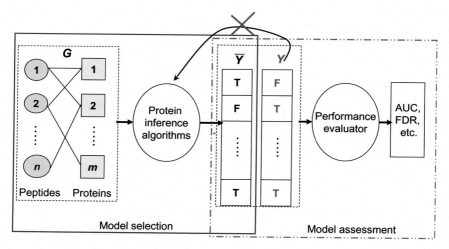

Figure 5.8 The correct and incorrect procedure for assessing the performance of protein inference algorithms. In model selection, we cannot use any ground truth information that should only be visible in the model assessment stage. Otherwise, we may overestimate the actual performance of inference algorithms.

positive if it comes from the target database and as a false positive otherwise. Therefore, the set of target/decoy labels is equivalent to the set of ground truth labels in this context. If we incautiously use the target-decoy information in both the model construction phase and validation phase of one protein inference algorithm, such overfitting in model selection will lead to an overestimation of its actual performance.

The fact that over-fitting at the level of model selection can have a very substantial deleterious effect in performance evaluation has been widely discussed and recognized in data mining fields and bioinformatics societies. In protein inference, we will face the same problem as well. Therefore, people should be aware of such risk in the future comparison when developing new protein inference algorithms.

5.7 Discussion and future perspective

Protein identification is one of most important problems in shotgun proteomics. Because proteins are more biologically relevant than peptides, it is critical to accurately infer all proteins present in the sample from identified peptides. However, such protein inference problem is still far from being resolved. This is because several technical challenges remain unsolved [4]: the identification coverage problem, the identification ambiguity problem, and the identification validation problem.

Identification coverage problem: Because of the complexity of proteomics data and the limitations of existing peptide identification algorithms, most tandem mass spectra in a typical proteomics experiment cannot be recognized confidently. As a result, only a subset of peptides present in the sample will be identified. This will lead to the exclusion of proteins that have no constituent peptides being identified in the protein inference step. Therefore, some truly present proteins will not be included in the identification results.

Identification ambiguity problem: The ambiguity in protein inference primarily comes from two sources: degenerate peptides (peptides that are shared by more than proteins) and one-hit wonders (proteins that have only one identified peptide). It is generally very difficult to determine which proteins are truly present in the sample if they share the same set of peptides or have only one constituent peptide identified.

Identification validation problem: One of the major problems in computational proteomics is the lack of widely accepted theoretical estimates of statistical significance of protein identifications. The Proteomics Publication Guidelines recommend the use of target-decoy strategy to validate protein identifications. Indeed, if the statistical significance of protein identifications can be estimated accurately in a decoy-free manner, the search in decoy database is not necessary.

In summary, more research efforts still should be devoted to the protein inference problem before the above technical challenges can be solved.

References

[1] A.M. Altelaar, J. Munoz, A.J. Heck, Next-generation proteomics: towards an integrative view of proteome dynamics, Nat. Rev. Genet. 14 (1) (2012) 35–48.

[2] M.S. Kim, et al., A draft map of the human proteome, Nature 509 (7502) (2014) 575–581.

[3] T. Huang, Z. He, A linear programming model for protein inference problem in shotgun proteomics, Bioinformatics 28 (22) (2012) 2956–2962.

[4] T. Huang, J. Wang, W. Yu, Z. He, Protein inference: a review, Brief. Bioinform. 13 (5) (2012) 586–614.

[5] C. Zhao, D. Liu, B. Teng, Z. He, BagReg: protein inference through machine learning, Comput. Biol. Chem. (2015).

[6] T. Huang, H. Gong, C. Yang, Z. He, ProteinLasso: a Lasso regression approach to protein inference problem in shotgun proteomics, Comput. Biol. Chem. 43 (2013) 46–54.

[7] R. Tibshirani, Regression shrinkage and selection via the Lasso, J. R. Stat. Soc. Ser. B (Methodol.) 58 (1) (1996) 267–288.

[8] Y. Zhang, Clustering Algorithm for Mixed Type Data and Its Application, Master's Dissertation, Dalian University of Technology, 2013 (in Chinese).

[9] B. Teng, T. Huang, Z. He, Decoy-free protein-level false discovery rate estimation, Bioinformatics 30 (5) (2014) 675–681.

[10] J.D. Storey, R. Tibshirani, Statistical significance for genomewide studies, Proc. Natl. Acad. Sci. U.S.A. 100 (16) (2003) 9440–9445.

PPI network inference from AP-MS data

6

6.1 Introduction to protein–protein interactions

Proteins mediate their functions physically by interacting with each other in stable or transient multiprotein complexes of distinct composition. To understand the diverse and dynamic proteome, it is necessary to construct the underlying networks of physical interactions. Moreover, proteins can interact with other molecules, such as metabolites, lipids, and nucleic acids. These complexes have essential roles in regulatory processes and cellular functions. Therefore, the construction and analysis of such interactome networks will provide important insights into the global organization of cellular systems.

There are two main types of high-throughput experimental methods for identifying protein–protein interactions (PPIs): yeast two-hybrid (Y2H) and affinity purification mass spectrometry (AP-MS).

Y2H primarily detects direct PPIs and can quickly screen large numbers of such interactions. Users often regard data from Y2H experiments as the proof of a direct interaction. However, the quality of Y2H data sets has been controversial because different Y2H systems can generate markedly different interactions in the same interactome. This is because false positives do occur when yeast proteins act as a bridge between two indirectly interacting proteins.

Recently, the combination of large-scale affinity purification (AP) with mass spectrometry (MS) is widely used to detect and characterize protein complexes. In AP-MS, a protein of interest ("bait") is affinity captured and then followed by MS to identify its interaction partners ("prey"). AP-MS can delineate the dynamics of interactions at different conditions to determine protein complex compositions.

6.2 AP-MS data generation

In a typical AP/MS experiment, selected proteins of interest ("baits") are purified along with their interactors ("preys") through one or more AP steps, as illustrated in Figure 6.1. Proteins in the affinity purified sample are digested into peptides with protease such as trypsin. The mixtures of peptides are separated using liquid chromatography coupled online to a mass spectrometer. Eluting peptides are ionized, transferred into a gas phase, and selected peptide ions are further fragmented to generate tandem mass spectra. These acquired spectra are used to identify peptides and proteins. The output data from such an AP/MS experiment is the bait protein and its possible interaction partners (prey proteins), and each protein can also be associated with its abundance information that is provided by the protein quantification method.

Data Mining for Bioinformatics Applications. http://dx.doi.org/10.1016/B978-0-08-100100-4.00006-5

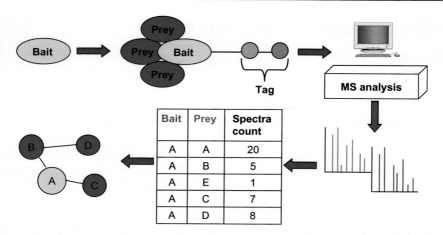

Figure 6.1 A typical AP-MS workflow for constructing PPI network. A typical AP-MS study performs a set of experiments on bait proteins of interest, with the goal of identifying their interaction partners. In each experiment, a bait protein is first tagged and expressed in the cell. Then, the bait protein and their potential interaction partners (prey proteins) are affinity purified using AP. The resulting proteins (both bait and prey proteins) are digested into peptides and passed to tandem mass spectrometer for analysis. Peptides are identified from the MS/MS spectra with peptide identification algorithms and proteins are inferred from identified peptides with protein inference algorithms. In addition, the label-free quantification method such as spectral counting is typically used to estimate the protein abundance in each experiment. Such pull-down bait–prey data from all AP-MS runs are used to filter contaminants and construct the PPI network.

Intuitively, each bait–prey protein pair should interact directly with others. In practice, however, there are a large number of false-positive interactions, where a prey protein can be either a contaminant or can interact with the bait indirectly.

6.3 Data collection and preprocessing

To conduct the PPI network, raw AP-MS data or preprocessed data need to be collected first. To date, many such AP-MS data sets are available online for academic use. Most of these public data sets have been preprocessed, in which the identified bait–prey pairs from raw MS data are provided to users. That is, the users need not perform preprocessing steps such as peptide identification and protein inference to obtain the bait–prey list. Table 6.1 lists some online AP-MS data resources that have been used in some recent studies.

6.4 Modeling with different data mining techniques

Generally, PPIs can be divided into two major types [1]: co-complex interactions and physical interactions. A protein complex is a group of proteins that interact with each other at the same location and time. The protein pair of co-complex interaction

Table 6.1 Some AP-MS data sets available online

Reference	URL
[2]	http://kroganlab.ucsf.edu/links.html
[3]	http://www.nature.com/nmeth/journal/v8/n1/abs/nmeth.1541.html
[4]	http://www.nature.com/nature/journal/v481/n7381/abs/nature10719.html
[5]	http://pubs.acs.org/doi/suppl/10.1021/pr201185r
[6]	http://www.sciencedirect.com/science/article/pii/S0092867409005030

interacts with each other in the formation of a complex. That is, if two proteins belong to the same complex (they do not have direct physical contact), then they have the co-complex interaction relationship. Unlike co-complex interactions, the physical interaction represents a direct biophysical interaction between two proteins, that is, two proteins are linked by an edge in the PPI network.

To construct the PPI network, either co-complex interactions or physical interactions can be used as the edges to connect protein nodes. Therefore, the key problem in the network inference from AP-MS data is how to accurately predict co-complex interactions and physical interactions. From the viewpoint of data mining, there are several different modeling approaches for such an interaction prediction task.

6.4.1 A correlation mining approach

The problem of interaction prediction from bait–prey data can be modeled as a correlation/association mining problem. The following computational framework can be used to illustrate most existing algorithms in this category.

First, the original AP-MS data are transformed into a type-value table. Here we use one simple example to illustrate this procedure, where a preprocessed bait–prey data set is given in Figure 6.2. In this sample data, there are six purifications where each selected bait protein captures a list of prey proteins. The transformed type-value table is shown in Table 6.2, where rows correspond to purifications, and each column represents the presence status of a specific protein in the corresponding purification. Note that the protein type (bait vs. prey) and the protein abundance information (e.g., spectral count) can also be recorded as the associated information with each cell in the table.

Based on the transformed table, the interaction prediction between different proteins could be modeled as the problem of pair-wise correlation mining among different features. These methods differ in several ways: the correlation measure used and the information used in the correlation calculation.

In Ref. [7], the Dice coefficient (DC) is used to measure the correlation between two proteins. More precisely, the interaction score between two proteins i and j is defined as: $2O_{ij}/(2O_{ij}+O_i+O_j)$, where O_{ij} is the number of times that both proteins i and j are 1s in the table, and O_i and O_j represent the number of times that only protein i is 1 and only protein j

Purification 1		
Bait	**Prey**	**Spectra count**
A	A	41
A	B	16
A	C	31
A	D	19
A	E	15

Purification 2		
Bait	**Prey**	**Spectra count**
B	B	20
B	F	5
B	G	1
B	C	7
B	A	18

Purification 3		
Bait	**Prey**	**Spectra count**
C	C	5
C	A	8
C	D	15
C	E	2
C	H	1

Purification 4		
Bait	**Prey**	**Spectra count**
D	D	30
D	E	67
D	F	1
D	G	33
D	H	3

Purification 5		
Bait	**Prey**	**Spectra count**
E	E	22
E	F	15
E	D	11
E	B	3
E	C	1

Purification 6		
Bait	**Prey**	**Spectra count**
F	F	25
F	A	18
F	G	5
F	E	12
F	D	18

Figure 6.2 A sample AP-MS data set with six purifications.

Table 6.2 **The transformed type-value table of the sample data in Figure 6.2**

	A	**B**	**C**	**D**	**E**	**F**	**G**	**H**
1	1 (b, 41)	1 (p, 16)	1 (p, 31)	1 (p, 19)	1 (p, 15)	0	0	0
2	1 (p, 18)	1 (b, 20)	1 (p, 7)	0	0	0	1 (p, 1)	0
3	1 (p, 8)	0	1 (b, 5)	1 (p, 15)	1 (p, 2)	0	0	1 (p, 1)
4	0	0	0	1 (b, 30)	1 (p, 67)	1 (p, 1)	1 (p, 33)	1 (p, 3)
5	0	1 (p, 3)	1 (p, 3)	1 (p, 11)	1 (b, 22)	1 (p, 15)	0	0
6	1 (p,18)	0	0	1 (p, 18)	1 (p, 12)	1 (b, 25)	1 (p, 5)	0

In the new data set, there are six samples and eight features. In each cell, 1 (0) denotes that the protein is present (absent) in the corresponding purification. In addition, the protein type and protein abundance information can be associated with each cell if its value is 1. Here b and p denote that the protein in the purification is a bait protein and a prey protein, respectively.

is 1, respectively. For instance, the interaction score based on DC is 4/7 for protein A and protein B in Table 6.2. Clearly, this method ignores both the bait/prey information and the protein abundance information in its scoring function.

Figure 6.3 shows the predicted PPI network when DC is used as the correlation measure with a cut-off threshold of 0.5.

In Ref. [8], the socio-affinity (SA) scoring method is proposed, which incorporates the protein type into the correlation calculation procedure. More precisely, the

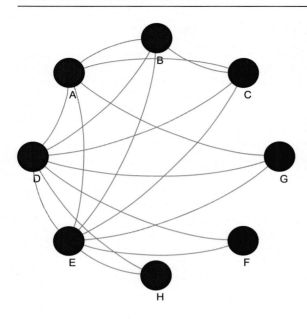

Figure 6.3 The PPI network constructed from the sample data. Here DC is used as the correlation measure and the score threshold is 0.5, that is, a protein pair is considered to be a true interaction if the DC score is above 0.5. In the figure, the width of the edge that connects two proteins is proportional to the corresponding DC score.

correlation score between two proteins i and j is composed of three parts: (1) the correlation score when protein i is the bait; (2) the correlation score when protein j is the bait; and (3) the correlation score when both protein i and protein j are not the bait. For example, if SA is used to calculate the association between protein A and protein B in Table 6.2, then the samples in Table 6.2 are divided into three sets: $\{1\}$, $\{2\}$, and $\{3,4,5,6\}$. The correlation score is first calculated for each subset and then the final score is the sum of three component scores.

The protein abundance information can be used in calculating the interaction score as well. In Ref. [9], the correlation of two proteins is defined in terms of the cosine-distance between their columns:

$$\text{sim}(i,j) = \frac{\sum_{k=1}^{n} x_{ki} x_{kj}}{\sqrt{\sum_{k=1}^{n} x_{ki}^2} \sqrt{\sum_{k=1}^{n} x_{kj}^2}}, \tag{6.1}$$

where $x_{ki}(x_{kj})$ is the protein abundance of the ith (jth) protein in the kth purification and n is number of total purifications. For instance, the cosine-distance between protein A and protein B in Table 6.2 is calculated as:

$$\frac{(41 \times 16 + 18 \times 20 + 8 \times 0 + 0 \times 0 + 0 \times 1 + 1 \times 0)}{\sqrt{(41^2 + 18^2 + 8^2 + 0^2 + 0^2 + 1^2)} \sqrt{16^2 + 20^2 + 0^2 + 0^2 + 1^2 + 0^2}} = 0.87$$

6.4.2   A discriminative pattern mining approach

In addition to the experimental data for bait proteins, AP-MS data often contain negative controls, in which the preys are likely to be contaminants because the tagged bait is not expressed. When the negative controls are available, it is possible to directly identify noninteracting bait–prey pairs from the perspective of discriminative pattern mining.

In Ref. [10], the protein expressions obtained from specific experiments are compared with the protein expressions obtained from negative control experiments to determine if a prey protein is a contaminant, that is, if the corresponding bait–prey pair is not a true interaction pair.

For m identified proteins and n purifications, let x_{ki} represent the normalized spectral abundance factor (NSAF) of the kth protein in the ith experiment. The vector $[x_{k1}, x_{k2},\ldots,x_{kn}]$ is defined as "protein vector." Similarly, let y_{ki} represent the NSAF value of kth identified protein in the ith control purification of negative controls. Then, the vector $[y_{k1}, y_{k2},\ldots,y_{kn}]$ represents the negative control protein vector. For each protein with two protein vectors, the vector magnitude (α) is calculated as:

$$\alpha = \sqrt{\frac{\langle y, y \rangle}{\langle x, x \rangle}} = \sqrt{\frac{y_{k1}^2 + y_{k2}^2 + \cdots + y_{kn}^2}{x_{k1}^2 + x_{k2}^2 + \cdots + x_{kn}^2}}. \tag{6.2}$$

If $\alpha \geq 1$, then the protein was more abundant in the negative controls than in the specific experiments. Hence, a protein with $\alpha \geq 1$ can be considered as a contaminant since it is "over-expressed" in the negative controls.

6.5   Validation

Based on whether one is using the additional reference database, there are two commonly used strategies for validating the constructed PPI networks. In the first strategy, the predicted network and the gold standard database are used as the input. Usually the PPIs in the reference database are collected from multiple sources and are postprocessed to remove erroneous interactions. In some databases, the interactions are further classified according to the type of interactions: physical interactions and co-complex interactions. Table 6.3 shows some available databases that are used for interaction validation. According to these databases, the predicted interactions can be evaluated through some standard performance indices such as accuracy and false discovery rate.

The database-based approach is probably the most widely used method for validating the interaction prediction results. This method is very accurate if the database is complete and all stored interactions in the database are valid. However, most databases are still not complete so far. Meanwhile, there may be some invalid interaction entries in the database. For some species or organisms, such a database-based validation approach is not applicable because there is still no gold standard database available in the literature.

Table 6.3 **Some high-quality protein–protein interaction database available online**

Database	URL
MIPS	http://mips.helmholtz-muenchen.de/proj/ppi/
BioGrid	http://biodata.mshri.on.ca/grid/servlet/Index
HPRD	http://www.hprd.org/
IntAct	http://www.ebi.ac.uk/intact/
DIP	http://dip.doe-mbi.ucla.edu/dip/Download.cgi
MINT	http://cbm.bio.uniroma2.it/mint/
HINT	http://hint.yulab.org

Alternatively, the database-free method does not need a gold standard database, which uses the predicted interactions and original AP-MS data set as the input. Generally, such database-free approaches have the following steps, as described in Figure 6.4:

1. The first step is to generate multiple simulated data sets that have the same characteristics as the original AP-MS data. Here the null hypothesis is: each bait captures a list of preys randomly. Under this null hypothesis, many simulated data sets can be created by randomly swapping two prey proteins from different baits. Hence, these simulated data sets are statistically comparable to the original one.
2. Then, PPIs are predicted on these random data sets with the algorithm to be evaluated. That means the original interaction prediction method should be repetitively executed many times.
3. Finally, the family-wise error rate or false discovery rate can be obtained by comparing the original prediction result with those generated from the simulated data sets.

6.6 Discussion and future perspective

The fast generation of AP-MS data makes it possible to find true PPIs with data mining methods. However, the data analysis problem has some special characteristics that are different from standard data mining issues and poses some new computational challenges, as we discuss below.

It is a very natural idea to model the interaction prediction problem as a pair-wise correlation mining issue. That is, the cooccurrence correlation between two proteins across the purifications is used to measure their interaction strength. However, such a strategy relies on the assumption that there are a sufficient number of purifications so that interacting proteins can cooccur frequently. Currently, small-to-intermediate scale AP-MS data sets are becoming increasingly popular, in which we may observe the cooccurrence between a tagged bait protein and a prey protein only once. This makes it unfeasible to employ traditional correlation mining techniques in the context of small-to-intermediate scale AP-MS experiments. Therefore, some new correlation mining formulations should be presented to handle such a distinct data analysis problem.

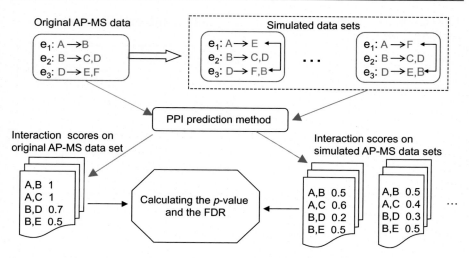

Figure 6.4 An illustration of database-free method for validating the interaction prediction results. Under the null hypothesis that each bait protein captures a prey protein is a random event, some simulated data sets are generated such that they are comparable to the original one. Then, an empirical *p*-value representing the probability that an original interaction score for a protein pair would occur in the random data sets by chance can be calculated. Finally, the false discovery rate is calculated according to these *p*-values.

Even for large-scale AP-MS data sets, it is still a challenging problem to determine how to assign weights to different protein types automatically in the correlation calculation procedure. The SA method [8] solves this problem by dividing the data into different parts according to if one of two proteins has been tagged as bait. This strategy is very effective in practice. However, it is probably not the best solution. New methods that can determine the weights of different protein types in a mathematically sound manner should be developed in the future.

Furthermore, current interaction prediction algorithms can only detect interaction between proteins that cooccur in the same purification. Those proteins, which never occur in the same purification but may interact with each other, are ignored. To fulfill this void, one feasible solution is to use the indirect association mining technique to find such kinds of protein interactions.

References

[1] B. Teng, C. Zhao, X. Liu, Z. He, Network inference from AP-MS data: computational challenges and solutions. Brief. Bioinform. (2014), http://dx,doi.org/10.1093/bib/bbu038.
[2] S.R. Collins, P. Kemmeren, X.C. Zhao, et al., Toward a comprehensive atlas of the physical interactome of *Saccharomyces cerevisiae*, Mol. Cell. Proteomics 6 (3) (2007) 439–450.

[3] H. Choi, B. Larsen, Z.Y. Lin, et al., SAINT: probabilistic scoring of affinity purification-mass spectrometry data, Nat. Methods 8 (2011) 70–73.

[4] S. Jager, P. Cimermancic, N. Gulbahce, et al., Global landscape of HIV-human protein complexes, Nature 481 (7381) (2012) 365–370.

[5] H. Choi, T. Glatter, M. Gstaiger, et al., SAINT-MS1: protein-protein interaction scoring using label-free intensity data in affinity purification-mass spectrometry experiments, J. Proteome Res. 11 (4) (2012) 2619–2624.

[6] M.E. Sowa, E.J. Bennett, S.P. Gygi, et al., Defining the human deubiquitinating enzyme interaction landscape, Cell 138 (2) (2009) 389–403.

[7] B. Zhang, B.H. Park, T. Karpinets, et al., From pull-down data to protein interaction networks and complexes with biological relevance, Bioinformatics 24 (7) (2008) 979–986.

[8] A.C. Gavin, P. Aloy, P. Grandi, et al., Proteome survey reveals modularity of the yeast cell machinery, Nature 440 (7084) (2006) 631–636.

[9] J. Kutzera, H.C.J. Hoefsloot, A. Malovannaya, et al., Inferring protein–protein interaction complexes from immunoprecipitation data, BMC Res. Notes 6 (2013) 468.

[10] M.E. Sardiu, Y. Cai, J. Jin, et al., Probabilistic assembly of human protein interaction networks from label-free quantitative proteomics, Proc. Natl. Acad. Sci. U.S.A. 105 (5) (2008) 1454–1459.

Protein complex identification from AP-MS data

7

7.1 An introduction to protein complex identification

In Chapter 6, we discussed some novel computational algorithms for predicting interactions that draw the raw bait–prey data one step closer to the target interactomes. However, each protein often carries out its functions by working as a member of a protein complex. A *protein complex* is a collection of proteins that interact with each other at the same time and location, and which has essential roles in regulatory processes, cellular functions, and signaling cascades. Therefore, it is critical to organize the filtered (or even unfiltered) interaction data into protein complexes. As a result, the detection of protein complexes is another important problem in the analysis of the AP-MS data.

Computationally, the problem of protein complexes detection is to find collections of protein groups, where proteins in each group tightly cooperate with each other. Intuitively, if two proteins belong to the same complex, then they should frequently cooccur together (directly or indirectly) in the AP-MS data.

7.2 Data collection and data preprocessing

Existing protein complex detection methods can be divided into two categories according to the input data [1]. First, some methods detect protein complexes from an established PPI network, which is generated by connecting protein pairs that interact with each other. Here the interaction relationship between different proteins is obtained from the interaction prediction methods listed in Chapter 6. Alternatively, other methods detect complexes from original AP-MS data directly. These methods usually model the AP-MS data as a bipartite graph in which the two sets of vertices are the set of baits and the set of preys, respectively.

7.3 Modeling: A graph clustering framework

From the viewpoint of data mining, the protein complex detection problem is essentially a cluster analysis problem. Despite the seeming difference among existing methods with respect to the input data, clustering criterion, and algorithmic principle, these methods can be unified under a common *graph clustering* framework.

A *graph* is a data structure that is formed by a set of *vertices* and a set of *edges*, where each edge connects two vertices. Graph clustering is to find groups of related

Data Mining for Bioinformatics Applications. http://dx.doi.org/10.1016/B978-0-08-100100-4.00007-7

vertices in a graph, where the vertices within each group are highly connected whereas there are only few edges between different groups [2].

To solve the graph clustering issue, scholars from different disciplines have already proposed numerous methods. These methods can be divided into several different categories [3]: graph partitioning, hierarchical clustering, partitional clustering, spectral clustering, modularity-based methods, dynamic algorithms (e.g., random walk), clique percolation, methods based on statistical inference, among others. Roughly, each of existing protein complex detection methods can find its corresponding category in the area of graph clustering. In the following, several typical protein complex detection methods are used to illustrate this point.

7.3.1 The clique percolation approach

The clique percolation method is based on the concept that the internal edges of a cluster are likely to form cliques due to their high density [4]. This method has been widely applied to solve the protein complex identification problem, where protein complexes generally correspond to dense subgraphs or cliques of the network.

CACHET [5] is a typical clique percolation method for identifying protein complexes from AP-MS data. It models the AP-MS data as a bipartite graph in which the two vertex sets are the set of baits and the set of preys, respectively. Each edge between a bait node and a prey node represents the bait–prey relationship in the original data. This method mainly has three steps:

1. First, all maximal bicliques are generated from the bipartite graph based on the assumption that proteins within protein-complex cores are highly interactive.
2. Next, potential false positive bait–prey edges are removed from each biclique to generate a set of reliable bicliques. Because these reliable bicliques may share many common proteins, a maximal independent set of them are used as the so-called protein-complex cores.
3. Finally, attachment proteins are included into the cores to form protein complexes with core-attachment substructures.

Figure 7.1 presents an example of a bait–prey bipartite graph, where $\{B1, B2, B3, B4\}$ is the set of bait proteins and $\{P1, P2, P3, P4, P5, P6\}$ is the set of prey proteins. The number associated with each edge denotes the reliability score of the corresponding bait–prey interaction, which is generated from the interaction prediction methods in Chapter 6, such as SA. This example graph is used to depict how the CACHET method identifies protein complexes via clique percolation.

First, three maximal bicliques, $G1$, $G2$, and $G3$, are extracted from the bipartite graph, as shown in Figure 7.2. If a clique is considered to be reliable when the average reliability score of its edges is larger than a threshold, then only two bicliques, $C1$ and $C2$, are considered to be reliable (suppose the threshold is 0.7), and $C3$ is discarded. Because $C1$ and $C2$ overlap with each other significantly, only $C1$ is finally reported as a protein-complex core.

Finally, the protein complex is identified by including bait protein $B3$ as the attachment of protein-complex core $C1$, as shown in Figure 7.3.

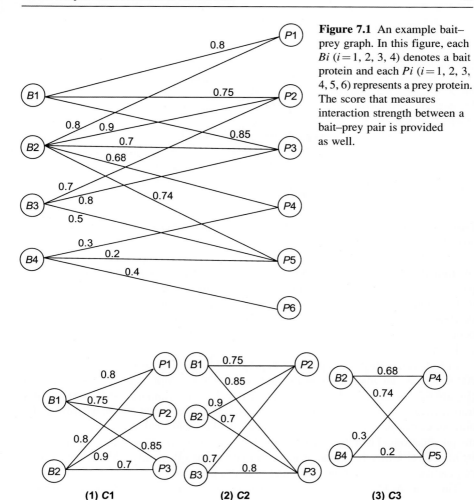

Figure 7.1 An example bait–prey graph. In this figure, each Bi ($i = 1, 2, 3, 4$) denotes a bait protein and each Pi ($i = 1, 2, 3, 4, 5, 6$) represents a prey protein. The score that measures interaction strength between a bait–prey pair is provided as well.

Figure 7.2 Three maximal bicliques are identified. Among these three bicliques, $C1$ and $C2$ are reliable and only $C1$ is finally reported as a protein-complex core.

7.3.2   The statistical inference method

Statistical inference deduces properties of data sets from a set of observations and hypotheses. When the data set is a graph, the clustering objective is to find a partition model that best fits the graph based on the connectivity patterns of vertices. In the context of protein complex identification, Bayesian inference is widely adopted in which observations (bait–prey graph) are used to estimate the probability that a given hypothesis is true.

There are two basic ingredients in Bayesian inference: the observed evidence and a statistical model with some parameters. Bayesian inference starts by writing the

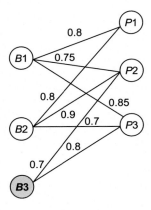

Figure 7.3 The final protein complex by including both the protein complex core $C1$ and an attachment $B3$.

likelihood that the observed evidence is generated by the model for a given set of parameters. The inference is performed to find parameters that maximize the posterior distribution of the parameters given the model and the evidence. Graph clustering can be considered to be a specific example of Bayesian inference problem, where the evidence is the graph structure and a hidden partition model that one wishes to infer along with some parameters.

In Ref. [6], a Bayesian approach is proposed to identify protein complexes from AP-MS data. To illustrate this method, we use the sample data set in Chapter 6 (Figure 6.2) as an example. As shown in Table 7.1, the original AP-MS data are first transformed into a binary purification matrix $\mathbf{U}$ with the size of $R \times N$, where R is the number of bait proteins and N is the number of all proteins that have once appeared in the purifications. Then, the corresponding adjacency matrix $\mathbf{M}$ in Table 7.2 is defined by $\mathbf{M} = \mathbf{U}^{\mathbf{T}}\mathbf{U}$, which is a symmetric $N \times N$ matrix. The ijth element, $\mathbf{M}_{ij}$, is the number of purifications in which protein i and protein j cooccur.

The element $\mathbf{M}_{ij}$ in the adjacency matrix can be regarded as the number of distinct "paths" between protein i and protein j discovered by the AP-MS experiment. For example, there are three paths between protein A and protein C and no path that

Table 7.1 The binary purification matrix

Protein	A	B	C	D	E	F	G	H
Bait A	1	1	1	1	1	0	0	0
Bait B	1	1	1	0	0	0	1	0
Bait C	1	0	1	1	1	0	0	1
Bait D	0	0	0	1	1	1	1	1
Bait E	0	1	1	1	1	1	0	0
Bait F	1	0	0	1	1	1	1	0

Table 7.2 **The adjacency matrix derived from Table 7.1**

	A	B	C	D	E	F	G	H
A	4	2	3	3	3	1	2	1
B	2	3	3	2	2	1	1	0
C	3	3	4	3	3	1	1	1
D	3	2	3	5	5	3	2	2
E	3	2	3	5	5	3	2	2
F	1	1	1	3	3	3	2	1
G	2	1	1	2	2	2	3	1
H	1	0	1	2	2	1	1	2

directly connects protein B and protein H. However, it is possible to reach protein H indirectly from protein B through their neighbors. For instance, B can connect with H via the path $B \rightarrow D \rightarrow H$. The number of distinct paths between two proteins via another protein can be directly obtained by the matrix product $\mathbf{MM}$. More generally, the number of paths from protein i to protein j of length l on the graph corresponds to the ijth element of the matrix $\mathbf{M}^l$. Therefore, the number of distinct paths with different lengths can be used to measure the "similarity" between two proteins. Based on this observation, the von Neumann diffusion kernel is used to evaluate the likelihood of two proteins belonging to the same complex in Ref. [6]:

$$K = \sum_{l=1}^{\infty} \gamma^{l-1} M^l = M(1 - \gamma M)^{-1}, \qquad (7.1)$$

where γ is a parameter (the diffusion factor) to make the effect of longer paths decay exponentially. The kernel can be normalized into [0, 1] in the following way:

$$S_{ij} = \frac{K_{ij}}{\sqrt{K_{ii}K_{jj}}}. \qquad (7.2)$$

Because the elements of von Neumann kernel matrix are between 0 and 1, this makes $\mathbf{S}_{ij}$ suitable as a probabilistic measure for evaluating the likelihood of two proteins belonging to the same complex.

To identify protein complexes, a binary matrix $\mathbf{Z}$ for protein complex membership is defined as well. Each entry z_{ci} in $\mathbf{Z}$ is a random variable, which indicates the membership of the ith protein in the cth complex. Note that the number of protein complexes is unknown in advance and one protein may belong to multiple complexes. The task here is to infer the unknown protein membership matrix $\mathbf{Z}$ from the observed AP-MS data.

Because the actual number of protein complexes is unknown, an infinite latent feature model is employed for protein complex membership identification [6]. Initially, the method starts with a finite model of C complexes, and then takes the limit as $C \to \infty$ to obtain the prior distribution over the binary matrix $\mathbf{Z}$.

If each protein belongs to a complex c with probability π_c, then the conditional probability $P(Z|\pi)$ is a product of binomial distributions:

$$P(Z|\pi) = \prod_{c=1}^{C} \prod_{i=1}^{N} P(z_{ci}|\pi_c) = \prod_{c=1}^{C} \pi_c^{n_c} (1 - \pi_c)^{N-n_c}, \tag{7.3}$$

where $n_c = \sum_{i=1}^{N} z_{ci}$ is the number of proteins in the cth complex.

If the prior distribution of π is a beta distribution $beta(\alpha/C, 1)$ with a model parameter α, then conditional distribution for any z_{ci} is:

$$P(z_{ci}|Z_{-i,c}) = \frac{n_{-i,c} + \alpha/C}{N + \alpha/C}, \tag{7.4}$$

where $Z_{-i,c}$ represents the set of all entries in $\mathbf{Z}$ except z_{ci}, and $n_{-i,c}$ is the number of proteins (excluding the ith protein) in the cth complex.

If we let $C \to \infty$, then the conditional distribution of z_{ci} becomes

$$P(z_{ci}|Z_{-i,c}) = \frac{n_{-i,c}}{N} \tag{7.5}$$

for any c such that $n_{-i,c} > 0$.

For the c's with $n_{-i,c} = 0$, the number of new complexes associated with this protein has a Poisson distribution:

$$P(v_i|Z_{-i,c}) = \left(\frac{\alpha}{N}\right)^{v_i} \frac{\exp\left(-\frac{\alpha}{N}\right)}{v_i!}, \tag{7.6}$$

where v_i is the expected number of new complexes.

For a given protein complex membership matrix $\mathbf{Z}$, the inner product of two protein column vectors $z_i^{\mathsf{T}} z_j$ can be used to check if protein i and protein j belong to the same complex. That is, two proteins are in the same complex if $z_i^{\mathsf{T}} z_j > 0$. Then, the likelihood can be evaluated as:

$$P(S|Z) = \prod_{\{ij:z_i^{\mathsf{T}} z_j > 0\}} \left(S_{ij}\right)^{z_i^{\mathsf{T}} z_j} \prod_{\{ij:z_i^{\mathsf{T}} z_j = 0\}} \left(1 - S_{ij}\right), \tag{7.5}$$

where $\mathbf{S}$ is the normalized von Neumann kernel matrix obtained from the AP-MS data.

According to the Bayes' theorem, the posterior distribution of the protein complex membership matrix $\mathbf{Z}$ is $P(Z|S)$, which is proportional to $P(S|Z)P(Z)$, where $P(S|Z)$ is given in (7.5), and $P(Z)$ is defined by the infinite latent feature model [6]. To carry out the inference, a Gibbs sampler with the following steps is used.

(1) Initialize **Z** randomly.
(2) For $t = 1$ to T
   (a) According to $P(z_{ci}|Z_{-i,c},S) \propto P(S|Z)P(z_{ci}|Z_{-i,c})$, sample z_{ci} for each i and each c with $n_{-i,c} > 0$.
   (b) According to $P(v_i|Z_{-i,c},S) \propto P(S|Z)P(v_i|Z_{-i,c})$, sample the number of new complexes for each i.
   (c) Save the sample **Z**

7.4 Validation

Essentially, the validation of detected protein complexes is a special issue of cluster validation. Due to the popularity of cluster analysis, the data mining literature has proposed many cluster validation techniques. These techniques fall into two categories: external validation methods and internal validation methods [7].

External validation methods evaluate a clustering result based on the knowledge of the correct class labels. These methods are only applicable when the true cluster structure is known in advance. In the context of protein complex detection, this means that the set of true protein complexes is available. The database-based validation approach presented in Chapter 6 is an external validation method, which can be applied to evaluate the protein complex identification results as well.

If no class label is available, the internal validation methods become appropriate. Internal validation techniques measure how well a given partition corresponds to the true cluster structure of the data based on the information intrinsic to the data alone. The database-free method (i.e., randomization method) in Chapter 6 does not use additional knowledge of known protein–protein interactions and protein complexes, which is a special internal validation method in the context of cluster analysis.

In addition to the randomization method discussed in Chapter 6, other types of internal measures can be used to assess the quality of detected protein complexes as well. These measures differ in their particular notions of clustering quality that they employ [7].

- *Compactness*: Intracluster homogeneity measures such as the average or maximum pairwise intracluster distances.
- *Separation*: Measures that quantify the degree of separation between individual clusters such as the average intercluster distance.
- *Compliance between a partition and distance information*: The degree to which distance information in the original data is preserved in the clustering result.

Note that the above internal measures are presented for general cluster analysis. In the context of graph clustering for protein complex detection, a novel notion of "distance" is needed to be clarified for a protein pair. For this purpose, the similarity score for measuring the affinity of protein–protein interactions such as the SA score in Chapter 6 can be used.

7.5   Discussion and future perspective

High-throughput technologies for generating large-scale AP-MS data have already become routine in most laboratories, while the accurate detection of protein complexes remains relatively immature. Hence, the development of effective computational approaches for detecting protein complexes is still needed. Although many new methods have been proposed to identify protein complexes from AP-MS data, many challenging problems need to be further investigated.

To date, computational methods for detecting protein complexes from the AP-MS data mostly focus on the high-density cluster, and protein complexes with low-density are always neglected. New clustering algorithms that are capable of finding such kinds of protein complexes should be developed.

During the past years, numerous algorithms have been developed in the literature of graph clustering. Unfortunately, only several types of graph clustering methods have been tested and applied to solve the protein complex detection problem. It would be plausible to investigate the feasibility of using other unexplored graph clustering algorithms so as to obtain more accurate protein complex identification result.

Existing algorithms for protein complex detection either focus on binary bait–prey data or quantitative AP-MS data. There are still no computational methods that can handle both types of data sets in a unified framework.

References

[1] B. Teng, C. Zhao, X. Liu, Z. He, Network inference from AP-MS data: computational challenges and solutions. Brief. Bioinform. (2014), http://dx.doi.org/10.1093/bib/bbu038.
[2] S.E. Schaeffer, Graph clustering, Comput. Sci. Rev. 1 (1) (2007) 27–64.
[3] S. Fortunato, Community detection in graphs, Phys. Rep. 486 (3–5) (2010) 75–174.
[4] G. Palla, I. Derényi, I. Farkas, T. Vicsek, Uncovering the overlapping community structure of complex networks in nature and society, Nature 435 (2005) 814–818.
[5] M. Wu, X. Li, C.K. Kwoh, et al., Discovery of protein complexes with core-attachment structures from tandem affinity purification (TAP) data, J. Comput. Biol. 19 (9) (2012) 1027–1042.
[6] W. Chu, Z. Ghahramani, R. Krause, D.L. Wild, Identifying protein complexes in high-throughput protein interaction screens using an infinite latent feature model, Pac. Symp. Biocomput. 11 (2006) 231–242.
[7] J. Handl, J. Knowles, D.B. Kell, Computational cluster validation in post-genomic data analysis, Bioinformatics 21 (15) (2005) 3201–3212.

Biomarker discovery

8.1 An introduction to biomarker discovery

As suggested by the Biomarkers Definitions Working Group, a *biomarker* is "a characteristic that is objectively measured and evaluated as an indicator of normal biological processes, pathogenic processes, or pharmacologic responses to a therapeutic intervention." With the advent of molecular biology and modern medicine, scientists begin to search for the biomarkers associated with disease processes at the molecular level. The molecular targets for biomarkers include biological molecules such as genes, transcripts, proteins, metabolites, and regulatory RNAs.

Generally, two basic styles are used in the research for biomarker discovery: hypothesis driven and discovery driven. The hypothesis-driven methods typically have clear candidate markers, which are usually identified during the study of disease processes. In contrast, the discovery-driven methods have no clear targets, which identify candidate biomarkers by analyzing the biological data sets through computational methods.

The advent of high throughput technologies has provided an unprecedented opportunity for identifying biomarkers from large-scale "omics" data in the discovery-driven style. Computationally, the biomarker discovery problem can be modeled as the problem of selecting features that can effectively distinguish cases from controls in a classification model. The biomarker discovery algorithms have been investigated for a long time, and numerous computational methods have been proposed from different research communities. In this chapter, the identification of biomarkers is studied from the viewpoint of data mining.

The major computational challenge in biomarker discovery is the so-called high-dimensional small-sample problem. That is, there are a huge number of genes or proteins/peptides that represent potential biomarkers in the data set. In contrast, the number of cases and controls is usually less than one thousand. As a result, the number of samples is significantly less than the number of features.

8.2 Data preprocessing

The discovery of biomarkers from high-throughput "omics" data is a very challenging task. It requires the collection and analysis of biological data in a quite complex pipeline. Typically, the discovery task is divided into different stages to reduce the complexity. To clarify this point, the biomarker discovery from mass spectrometry (MS) data is used as an example here to illustrate the preprocessing step and the analysis procedure.

MS has proved to be a useful tool for generating protein profiles of tissue, serum, and urine samples for case–control studies [1]. Ideally, the MS device should only generate peaks that are produced from ionized proteins or peptides. However, the

Data Mining for Bioinformatics Applications. http://dx.doi.org/10.1016/B978-0-08-100100-4.00008-9

acquired mass spectra contain not only true peaks that correspond to proteins or peptides of scientific interest but also noisy signals. Therefore, the following preprocessing steps should be conducted before the execution of core biomarker selection procedure, as presented in Figure 8.1.

1. *Feature extraction*: The first step is the extraction of "signals" or "features" from each spectrum. This involves many low-level signal processing tasks such as smoothing, peak detection, and peak quantification. Feature extraction is the most critical step in biomarker identification since all subsequent analysis steps use extracted features as input.
2. *Feature alignment*: Feature alignment establishes the correspondence among biological features extracted from different spectra. In other words, the aim of feature alignment is to produce a two-dimensional table that can be used in biomarker selection.
3. *Feature transformation (optional)*: A set of new features is created, where each new feature is obtained from the transformation or combination of old features. For instance, some methods (e.g., Ref. [2]) find a group of correlated proteins from the protein–protein interaction network, and then transform each group into a new feature for subsequent feature selection and classification. As shown in the example of Figure 8.2, the new feature T_2 is obtained by combining features F_3, F_5, and F_6.

8.3 Modeling

After the preprocessing step, the transformed data in the form of a two-dimensional table is used to generate a subset of features as markers. From the angle of data mining and machine learning, such a task is often modeled as a feature selection problem.

Generally, feature selection methods can be categorized based on how they are coupled to the classification model [3]. As shown in Figures 8.3–8.5, there are

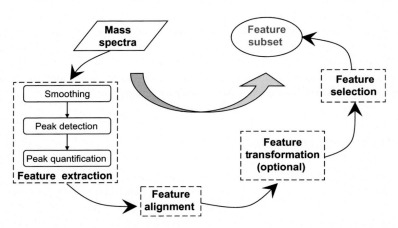

Figure 8.1 A typical data analysis pipeline for biomarker discovery from mass spectrometry data. In this workflow, there are three preprocessing steps: feature extraction, feature alignment, and feature transformation. After preprocessing the raw data, feature selection techniques are employed to identify a subset of features as the biomarker.

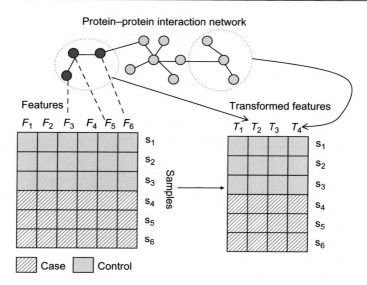

Figure 8.2 An illustration of feature transformation based on protein–protein interaction (PPI) information. The PPI information is used to find groups of correlated features in terms of proteins. These identified feature groups are transformed into a set of new features for biomarker identification.

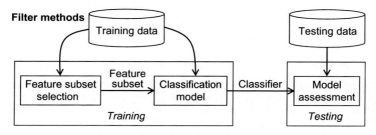

Figure 8.3 Filter methods for feature selection. In the filter method, the goodness of a feature subset is evaluated using only the intrinsic properties of the data.

generally three different types of feature selection methods: filter methods, wrapper methods, and embedded methods.

- *Filter methods*: The feature subset generation and evaluation is conducted as a preprocessing step, which is independent of the classification model used.
- *Wrapper methods*: The selection criterion of feature subset is determined by the performance of the classification model, which is strongly dependent on the specific classification method used.
- *Embedded methods*: The feature subset generation and evaluation is embedded as an integral part of the classification algorithm.

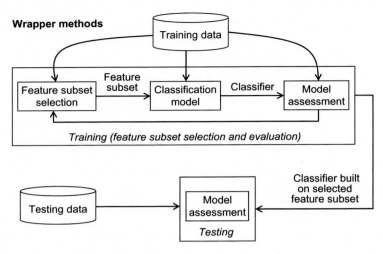

Figure 8.4 Wrapper methods for feature selection. In the wrapper method, the feature subset selection is based on the performance of a classification algorithm.

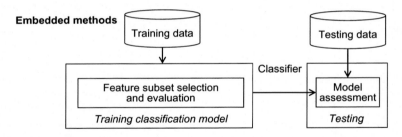

Figure 8.5 Embedded methods for feature selection. In the embedded method, the selection of feature subset is integrated with the construction of the classifier.

Among these methods, filter approaches are simple and flexible. Wrapper methods and embedded approaches directly optimize the classification performance during the feature selection process at the cost of incurring a high computational burden and probably over-fitting the classification model.

Here an unpublished feature selection method for biomarker discovery is introduced for the purpose of illustration. This method is named as *F*eature ranking using *B*inary *T*hreshold *C*lassifier (FBTC). It is a filter method, in which each feature is evaluated individually according to its classification capability estimated by a binary threshold classifier. The use of a binary threshold classifier in ranking features enables us to reduce the effect of variation in biological feature values, whereas evaluating each feature separately is computationally efficient.

Figure 8.6 illustrates the FBTC method, which outputs the ranking values of all *m* features. The basic idea is to evaluate each feature individually according to its

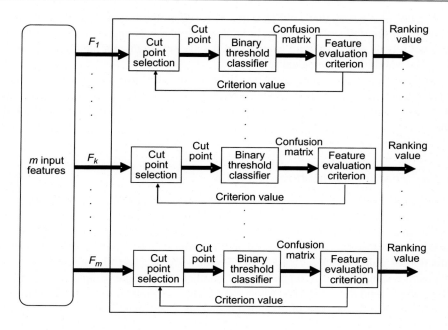

Figure 8.6 An illustration of the FBTC method.

classification power estimated by a binary threshold classifier. In the following, the details of this feature selection method are explained step by step.

8.3.1 Cut point selection

For a given feature F_k, we order all S sample values in the training set in a nondecreasing manner, that is, $F_k(X_1) \leq F_k(X_2) \leq \cdots \leq F_k(X_S)$. According to the procedure of the binary threshold classifier, it is sufficient to consider one cut point (e.g., $(F_k(X_h)+F_k(X_{h+1}))/2$) in each interval of $[F_k(X_h), F_k(X_{h+1})]$. In total, we only need to consider $S-1$ cut points for evaluation.

8.3.2 Binary threshold classifier

The basic idea of a binary threshold classifier on a numeric feature F_k is very simple. It consists of a cut point p_i and a target class c (1 corresponds to the positive class and 0 corresponds to the negative class). The decision function $BTC(X_h \mid p_i, c, F_k)$ is defined as:

$$BTC(X_h|p_i,c,F_k) = \begin{cases} c, & \text{if } F_k(X_h) > p_i \\ \bar{c}, & \text{if } F_k(X_h) \leq p_i \end{cases} \tag{8.1}$$

where $F_k(X_h)$ represents the feature value of a sample X_h and p_i denotes the threshold.

The use of a binary threshold classifier is based on the following considerations.

Why threshold classifier: A threshold classifier is robust against noise because it does not rely on precise feature values, which makes it suitable for handling the coefficient of variation in biological features.

Why binary classifier: The rationale can be discussed from two perspectives. First, it is natural to use a binary classifier because we are handling a binary classification problem (cancer vs. normal). Second, such a binary classifier is simple and easy to implement.

8.3.3 Feature evaluation criterion

Classification performances are typically evaluated using measures such as sensitivity and specificity. In the confusion matrix given in Table 8.1, cases (people have a certain disease) are considered as "positives" (class 1) and controls (people who have no that disease) are considered as "negatives" (class 0). In the horizontal direction of Table 8.1, $P = TP + FN$ and $N = FP + TN$, where P denotes the number of positive samples and N represents the number of negative samples. Vertically, $PP = TP + FP$ and $PN = FN + TN$, where PP denotes the number of predicted positives and PN denotes the number of predicted negatives. Correspondingly, some common evaluation metrics are defined in Table 8.2 as well.

Table 8.1 Confusion matrix defines four possible scenarios when classifying samples in the context of biomarker discovery

		Predicted class		
		Case	Control	Row total
Actual class	Case	True positives (*TP*)	False negatives (*FN*)	*P*
	Control	False positives (*FP*)	True negatives (*TN*)	*N*
Column total		*PP*	*PN*	*S*

Table 8.2 Performance metrics for evaluating classifiers

Names	Abbreviations and definitions
Specificity	$Spec = TN/N$
Sensitivity	$Sens = TP/P$
Positive predictive value	$PPV = TP/PP$
Negative predictive value	$NPV = TN/PN$
Accuracy	$ACC = (TP + TN)/S$
Balanced accuracy	$BACC = (Spec + Sens)/2$

We can use different measures in Table 8.2 to evaluate the importance of features. Here another more general measure is used, which is a function of measures in the confusion matrix:

$$U(p_i, c, F_k) = \max \left\{ TP_i^c - \pi_N FP_i^c, TN_i^c - \pi_P FN_i^c \right\}, \tag{8.2}$$

where π_N denotes the *penalty* of false positives and π_P is the *penalty* of false negatives. The subscript and superscript indicate that outcomes are from the condition of cut point p_i and target class c. In general, any value in the interval $[0, +\infty)$ is meaningful as a proper assignment for π_N and π_P.

The feature evaluation criterion is defined as:

$$FEC(F_k) = \arg \max_{p_i, c \in \{0, 1\}} U(p_i, c, F_k), \tag{8.3}$$

where p_i goes through $S - 1$ cut points to find the best classification result provided by this feature.

The setting of two penalty parameters is critical in feature ranking. Furthermore, several specific choices have clear practical implications. Suppose that the maximal value of $U(p_i, c, F_k)$ for feature F_k is achieved at the cut point p_i, at which the following properties can be observed.

- If $\pi_N = 1$ and $\pi_P = 1$, then the maximal *ACC* value is also achieved at the cut point p_i.
- If $\pi_N = P/N$ and $\pi_P = N/P$, then the maximal *BACC* value is also achieved at the cut point p_i.
- If $\pi_N = \pi_P \to +\infty$, then the maximum value of *PPV* or *NPV* is also achieved at the cut point p_i under the constraint of $NPV = 1$ or $PPV = 1$.

Clearly, the *FEC* criterion is closely related with common *ACC* and *BACC* measures by assigning certain values to π_N and π_P. In other words, *FEC* is a more general measure for feature ranking.

After ranking all features, we can select a subset of features with higher ranks and carry out classification using these features.

8.4   Validation

Besides the wet-lab validation through biological assays and clinical trials, several commonly used evaluation criteria are used for validating the reported biomarkers in the data-analytic phase of biomarker discovery.

1. *Classification performance*: One important goal of the biomarker discovery is to generate a subset of features that can accurately distinguish different classes such as the different stages of some diseases. Therefore, the prediction performance of the classification model built on the selected feature subset is an outstanding criterion. The most commonly used performance measure is the classification accuracy, which is defined as the percentage of correctly classified test samples. In some special cases, more concerns are given to class-specific performance measures such as sensitivity and specificity, which are defined as the proportion of correctly classified samples in the positive and the negative class, respectively.

2. *The size of feature subset*: To date, the number of candidate biomarkers that can be identified and validated for diagnostic purposes is rather limited. Therefore, most studies focus on biomarkers that are composed of a handful of features. In other words, the number of selected features should be as small as possible. Based on this fact, the number of selected features can serve as a criterion for the biomarker evaluation as well. In biomarker identification, minimizing the number of selected features might be even more important than improving the classification accuracy.

3. *Stability*: Traditionally, the classification accuracy is used as the major criterion for biomarker selection. In high-dimensional biological data, it can be observed that many different feature subsets have the same or similar predictive performance. If there is only one true biomarker, it is difficult to distinguish true biomarkers from false ones effectively only according to the classification performance. Therefore, the nonreproducibility of reported markers has become one major obstacle in biomarker discovery. Recently, the stability of a selected feature subset has become a new criterion for biomarker validation [4]. The stability of a feature subset is a good indicator of marker reproducibility. Although stability cannot override classification performance in the evaluation of candidate markers, it is a useful auxiliary criterion when the candidate feature subsets have similar predictive accuracy.

When the classification accuracy is used as the performance measure, the cross-validation approach is widely adopted for a rigorous evaluation. There are several variants of cross-validation in the literature. The k-fold cross-validation partitions the data into approximately k parts, in which one part is used for testing and another $k-1$ parts are used for feature selection and model training. The leave-one-out cross-validation takes only one sample as the testing sample and uses all remaining samples as the training samples.

To evaluate the stability of biomarkers (feature subset), one strategy is to randomly sample many subsets of the original training data. The feature selection method is performed on these subsamplings of the training data to check whether the target feature subset can be identified frequently. This procedure is illustrated in Figure 8.7.

8.5 Case study

In this section, the method in Ref. [5] is used as an example to illustrate the data analysis process in biomarker discovery. To identify biomarkers that can distinguish hepatocellular carcinoma (HCC) from cirrhosis, mass spectra from 84 HCC patients, 51 cirrhotic patients, and 80 healthy individuals are first generated.

In feature extraction, each mass spectrum was smoothed with the lowess smoothing method and was normalized by dividing its total ion current. Then, the slope of the peaks is used as the criterion for peak detection. The detected peaks correspond to target features in biomarker discovery.

In feature alignment, detected peaks from different samples are aligned together if their locations are no more than a given threshold.

In feature selection, a wrapper approach is exploited in which support vector machine (SVM) is used as the classifier. The proposed method reported a set of eight peaks as biomarkers. The SVM classifier built with these peaks achieved very

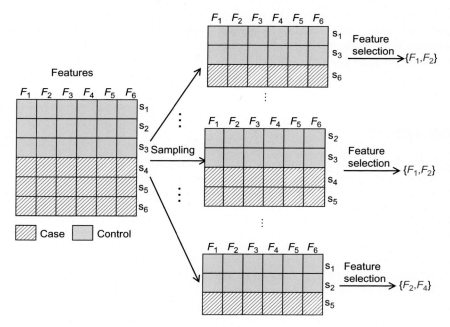

Figure 8.7 Stability evaluation by randomly sampling the original training data. Suppose multiple random subsets of the original training data set are generated. For each random subset of samples, the feature selection method is used to identify a feature subset. If the candidate biomarker (feature subset) identified from the original data has good stability, then it should occur frequently in the set of feature subsets obtained from the randomly selected data sets.

high classification accuracy in distinguishing HCC from cirrhosis in an independent testing data set.

8.6 Discussion and future perspective

During the past decades, feature selection methods have been used as the workhorse for identifying biomarkers in different applications. However, the biomarker discovery problem poses some new computational challenges that cannot be fully addressed by the traditional feature selection techniques. For instance, the stability of selected feature subset with respect to sampling variations has long been under-considered. As summarized in Ref. [4], there are already some stable feature selection methods for biomarker discovery in the literature. However, many data-analytical issues remain unsolved. For instance, how does one directly measure the stability of a feature subset? Is it possible to explicitly control the stability of a reported feature subset in the feature selection procedure?

The reason for the failure of identifying really useful clinical biomarkers from "omics" data sets of genes, transcripts, proteins, or other significant biological molecules is very complicated. One important factor is that the true relevant biological molecules cannot be captured and recorded in the data set to be analyzed for biomarker selection. In this case, it is impossible to discover biomarkers successfully. Therefore, besides developing more sophisticated biomarker identification algorithms, it is more critical to improve the data coverage of wet-lab technologies for profiling biological molecules.

References

[1] Z. He, R.Z. Qi, W. Yu, Bioinformatic analysis of data generated from MALDI mass spectrometry for biomarker discovery, Top. Curr. Chem. 331 (2013) 193–210.

[2] H.-Y. Chuang, E. Lee, Y.-T. Liu, D. Lee, T. Ideker, Network-based classification of breast cancer metastasis, Mol. Syst. Biol. 3 (2007) 140.

[3] M. Hilario, A. Kalousis, Approaches to dimensionality reduction in proteomic biomarker studies, Brief. Bioinform. 9 (2) (2008) 102–118.

[4] Z. He, W. Yu, Stable feature selection for biomarker discovery, Comput. Biol. Chem. 34 (4) (2010) 215–225.

[5] H. Ressom, R. Varghese, S. Drake, et al., Peak selection from MALDI-TOF mass spectra using ant colony optimization, Bioinformatics 23 (5) (2007) 619–626.

Conclusions

There can be no doubt that data mining is a cornerstone of modern bioinformatics. Over the past decades, data mining techniques have been successfully applied to solve many critical bioinformatics problems in life science. In this book, several examples are used to illustrate how to model a real bioinformatics problem as a data mining problem and then solve it by employing existing algorithms or developing new algorithms. Note that it is almost impossible to cover all bioinformatics problems in single book. It is my hope that this book can elicit further systematic research on data mining techniques for bioinformatics applications.

I would like to end this book with some general issues that should be further investigated to promote the success of data mining techniques in bioinformatics applications.

First, many bioinformatics problems in different applications are essentially the same data mining problem. For instance, numerous prediction problems in bioinformatics are concerned with categorizing biological sequences into different classes, which actually can be unified under the framework of sequence classification in data mining. Unfortunately, many research efforts have been devoted to each specific application, without the awareness of progress that has been made in other applications that are trying to solve the same computational problem. Therefore, these bioinformatics problems should be studied jointly, making it possible to investigate each bioinformatics issue from different perspectives. Such a wider range of view may enable a better understanding of our target bioinformatics problem and help us to devise better algorithms by combining elements from areas that would otherwise be considered as irrelevant.

Second, people have to borrow additional information from other data sources to solve the target data analysis problem in many bioinformatics applications. The integration of orthogonal data sources has become a common practice for handling bioinformatics issues that are hard to solve due to the lack of discriminative information in the data at hand. Although many successful stories have been reported and published, there are still no rigorous studies on the common data fusion strategies across different bioinformatics applications. In fact, the data fusion methods and algorithms in various seemingly different applications share the same underlying principle. The summarization and generalization of existing data fusion techniques will definitely be beneficial to the data mining practice in future bioinformatics applications.

Finally, but definitely not least, the assessment of data mining results in the context of bioinformatics applications is often problematic. This is primarily caused by the incompleteness and uncertainty of ground truth data. For instance, the set of true protein–protein interactions in many species are only partially known, and these known interactions are not all correct. If we have built a classifier for predicting unknown interactions, estimating the prediction performance of this classifier in an unbiased manner is a nontrivial issue. The same situation can be observed in many other bioinformatics applications as well. Therefore, the performance estimation problem in the context of incomplete and uncertain ground truth data must be thoroughly investigated in the future.

Index

Note: Page numbers followed by f indicate figures and t indicate tables.

Printed in the United States
By Bookmasters